TOP **10**
DEVON AND
CO KT-415-408

ROBERT ANDREWS

EYEWITNESS TRAVEL

Left **The Harbour Hotel** Centre **Ottery St Mary** Right **Circular houses in Veryan**

LONDON, NEW YORK,
MELBOURNE, MUNICH AND DELHI
www.dk.com

Design, Editorial and Picture Research by
Quadrum Solutions, Krishnamai, 33B, Sir
Pochkhanwala Road, Worli, Mumbai, India

Reproduced by Colourscan, Singapore
Printed and bound in China by
Leo Paper Products Ltd

First published in Great Britain in 2009 by
Dorling Kindersley Limited, 80 Strand,
London WC2R 0RL
A Penguin Company

**Copyright 2009 © Dorling
Kindersley Limited, London**

A CIP catalogue record is available from the
British Library.

ISBN 978 1 4053 3767 0

Within each Top 10 list in this book, no
hierarchy of quality or popularity is implied.
All 10 are, in the editor's opinion,
of roughly equal merit.

> **We're trying to be cleaner and greener:**
> • we recycle waste and switch things off
> • we use paper from responsibly managed
>   forests whenever possible
> • we ask our printers to actively reduce
>   water and energy consumption
> • we check out our suppliers' working
>   conditions – they never use child labour
> **Find out more about our values and
> best practices at www.dk.com**

Contents

Devon and Cornwall's Top 10

The information in this DK Eyewitness Top 10 Travel Guide is checked regularly.
Every effort has been made to ensure that this book is as up-to-date as possible at the time of
going to press. Some details, however, such as telephone numbers, opening hours, prices,
gallery hanging arrangements and travel information are liable to change. The publishers
cannot accept responsibility for any consequences arising from the use of this book, nor for
any material on third party websites, and cannot guarantee that any website address in this
book will be a suitable source of travel information. We value the views and suggestions of
our readers very highly. Please write to: Publisher, DK Eyewitness Travel Guides,
Dorling Kindersley, 80 Strand, London WC2R 0RL.

Left **Porthminster Beach, St Ives** Right **The Italianate Garden, Mount Edgcumbe**

Left **Padstow Harbour** Right **Powderham Castle**

Key to abbreviations
Adm *admission charge*

DEVON AND CORNWALL'S TOP 10

DEVON AND CORNWALL'S TOP 10

⟶10 Devon and Cornwall's Highlights

The Southwest peninsula holds some of Britain's most forbidding moorland, dramatic coastline and enticing beaches. Its history, stretching from Celtic to Victorian times, is strikingly illustrated in its castles and stately homes, while year-round, a range of outdoor activities and all-weather attractions provide entertainment and instruction for the whole family. Equally renowned for old-fashioned tranquillity and soul-stirring views, Devon and Cornwall provide the ideal canvas for the perfect holiday.

1 Lanhydrock
This impressive 17th-century mansion is filled with Jacobean art and Victorian furnishings. Immaculate gardens and sweeping parkland surround the house *(see pp8–9)*.

2 Eden Project
Conservation is made fun at this wide-ranging exploration of the plant world, dominated by two giant greenhouses. Summer concerts, winter ice-skating and several cafés and restaurants serving great food enhance its appeal *(see pp10–11)*.

3 Dartmoor
A range of activities is possible on this bleak expanse of moorland, which is complemented by grand houses and cosy villages sheltering thatched pubs *(see pp12–13)*.

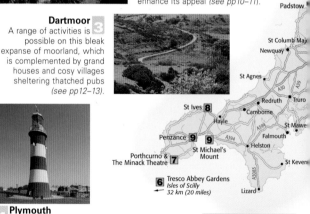

4 Plymouth
Enjoying a superb location, this seafaring city was the home port of the intrepid sailor Sir Francis Drake. It still preserves traces of the Elizabethan era. Within a short distance are palatial houses and country parks *(see pp14–15)*.

5 Exeter
Rising from the River Exe, the capital of Devon has a strong historical flavour, not least in its cathedral and other ancient monuments. It also has a buzzing and vibrant contemporary cultural life *(see pp18–21)*.

Padstow

St Columb Majɔ
Newquay

St Agnes

St Ives 8
Hayle
Redruth
Camborne
Truro

Penzance 9
St Michael's
Mount
A394
Falmouth
Helston
St Mawe

Porthcurno & 7
The Minack Theatre

6 Tresco Abbey Gardens
Isles of Scilly
← 32 km (20 miles)

Lizard

St Keverı

⟹ Preceding pages **A biome at the Eden Project**

7 Porthcurno and the Minack Theatre

Porthcurno has a range of outdoor attractions, including a sandy beach between high cliffs and the open-air Minack Theatre, hewn out of the rock *(see pp24–25)*.

6 Tresco Abbey Gardens

On a wind-blasted island in the middle of the Atlantic, this gracious garden of semi-tropical plants has been created within the walls of a ruined abbey *(see pp22–23)*.

8 St Ives

Home to the Tate St Ives gallery, this quirky seaside town has a thriving arts scene. Sandy beaches and excellent restaurants are further attractions here *(see pp26–27)*.

9 Penzance and St Michael's Mount

The region's most westerly town is home to two superb galleries and is close to St Michael's Mount, a fortified house crowning an island *(see pp28–29)*.

10 Padstow

Famous for its gourmet restaurants, this North Cornwall fishing port is also notable for its beaches, historic houses and a cycling and walking trail *(see pp30–31)*.

Devon and Cornwall's Top 10

🔟 Lanhydrock

This magnificent 17th-century mansion set in the Fowey Valley is one of England's grandest country houses. Built originally by a rich merchant, Sir Richard Robartes, it remained in the same family until the National Trust took it over in 1953. It was reconstructed in 1881 following a disastrous fire. Though parts of the Jacobean building survived – notably its famous Long Gallery – the dominant style is that of the High Victorian era. The warren of 50 visitable rooms offer a glimpse into life inside a stately pile, from the huge kitchens to Lady Robartes' boudoir.

1 Captain Tommy's Bedroom

This room is dedicated to Thomas Agar-Robartes, who died in the Battle of Loos in 1915. A suitcase kept on the cast-iron bed contains his personal items.

The gardens at Lanhydrock

🚗 It's a nice walk from the ticket booth to the house, but to get into the aristocratic spirit of Lanhydrock, take advantage of a vintage car service.

🍴 In the house, the Servants' Hall restaurant offers food, and there is a snack bar in the stables.

- Map D4
- Near Bodmin, Cornwall
- 01208 265950
- House: open mid-Mar–Sep: 11am–5:30pm Tue–Sun & national hols; Oct: 11am–5pm Tue–Sun; garden: open 10am–6pm daily
- Adm £9, child £4.50, family £22.50; grounds £5, child £2.50
- Vintage car service: adm £1.50, child 75p
- www.nationaltrust.org.uk

Top 10 Features

1. Captain Tommy's Bedroom
2. Woodland Walks
3. The Gardens
4. The Gatehouse
5. The Dining Room
6. The Billiard Room
7. The Nursery Wing
8. The Museum
9. The Long Gallery
10. St Hydrock Church

2 Woodland Walks

The woods and parkland of the estate are lovely to explore. Here, you can enjoy the exuberant birdlife and, in spring, brilliant expanses of bluebells *(above)* and daffodils.

3 The Gardens

The clipped yew trees and geometric flower-beds are striking *(below)*, but it is the magnolias in the shrub garden for which the gardens are most renowned.

Discounts are offered to visitors who arrive by bicycle or public transport.

The Gatehouse
4 This impressive, pinnacled structure was built in around 1650. The main room on the upper storey was used to entertain ladies while the men hunted. It now holds temporary exhibitions.

The Dining Room
5 Decorated with blue and gilt wallpaper designed by William Morris, the dining room is dominated by a table set for a formal meal as it would have been in Victorian times.

The Billiard Room
6 This spacious room exudes the spirit of the leisured life of the gentry with its billiard table *(above)* and tiger skin set against oak-panelling. Old school photos and other mementos line the walls.

The Nursery Wing
7 A whole suite of rooms was set aside for bringing up the younger family members. The nursery itself is crowded with a large doll's house and rocking horse among other toys *(above)*.

The Museum
8 Entered from the courtyard, a panelled room holds quirky items such as a carrying case for poultry, and family photos and albums depicting war casualties.

The Long Gallery
9 Lanhydrock's pièce de résistance occupying the north wing's entire first floor, is famed for its remarkable plaster ceiling which illustrates stories from the Old Testament.

St Hydrock Church
10 Dedicated to an Irish missionary, the church *(right)* adjoining the house dates from the 15th century. A plaster panel in the north aisle displays the arms of King James I, dated 1621.

Below Stairs

More than any other house of its period, Lanhydrock provides an intriguing insight into how a grand mansion actually operated. At the heart of the building is the refectory-like kitchen, with its elaborate ranges and spits. Passages lead from here to sculleries, larders, a bakehouse and a dairy. At the top of the house, the modest servants' quarters are a stark contrast to the lavish bedrooms of the owners.

🔟 Eden Project

A china clay pit transformed to house two giant conservatories and an extensive area of outdoor beds, the Eden Project is an innovative exploration of the plant world and man's interaction with it. Although it is the grand spectacle of the place that grabs the attention, the Eden Project has a serious agenda, aimed at alerting us to the fragility of Earth's ecosystem, through talks and workshops organized around the year. The educational element, however, does not stifle the sense of fun. In summer, this is one of the region's best venues for open-air concerts, while the arena becomes an ice rink in winter.

An orchid at the Rainforest Biome

Outdoor seating at one of Eden's cafés

🍂 Eden can be taxing on the feet, but the Land Train provides some relief – especially for the ascent to the exit.

🍴 There is no need to bring food here – Eden has many good-quality restaurants and cafés.

- Map D4
- Bodelva, Cornwall
- 01726 811911
- Open mid-Mar–Oct: 9:30am–6pm; Aug: closes 8pm Tue, Wed & Thu; Nov–mid-Mar: 10am–4:30pm; last adm 90 min before closing
- Adm £15, child £5, seniors £10, students £7, family £36; reduced adm after 4:30pm in summer: adults adm £9; seniors £7; child free
- www.edenproject.com

Top 10 Features

1. Visitor Centre
2. Rainforest Biome
3. Mediterranean Biome
4. Eden Sessions
5. Eden's Restaurants
6. The Mechanical Theatre
7. Eden's Artworks
8. Outside Biome
9. The Core
10. Bulb Mania

Visitor Centre

Adorned with sculptures, such as Heather Jansch's *Driftwood Horse* made from driftwood and cork, the Visitor Centre, a lofty viewpoint at the top of the pit, gives a taste of the marvels to come. From here, the full scale of the place becomes apparent.

Rainforest Biome

Hot and steamy with a waterfall coursing through it, this luxuriant biome *(left)* recreates a tropical climate for plants and rainforest flowers from West Africa, Amazonia and Malaysia.

Mediterranean Biome

The smaller of the two indoor biomes *(right)* houses plants from the Mediterranean, South Africa and southwestern America. Exhibits include orange trees, olives and vividly coloured flowers.

Eden Sessions
4 The crowd-pulling "Eden Sessions" held in summer have included memorable gigs by the Kaiser Chiefs, KT Tunstall *(above)* and lesser-known world music artists.

Eden's Restaurants
5 Award-winning restaurants here offer global cuisine prepared from locally sourced ingredients. Dishes include everything from enchiladas to char-grilled halloumi cheese and even Cornish tea. Restaurants include the Apple Café, Jo's Café and Zzub Zzub.

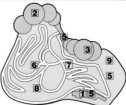

The Mechanical Theatre
6 Ecological issues are given an offbeat interpretation in shows staged here, and feature acts by robotic puppets, with animation filling in the gaps.

Eden's Artworks
7 The artworks at Eden include specially commissioned temporary exhibits and permanent displays, such as a giant bee *(below)* and Dionysian figures in the Mediterranean Biome.

Outside Biome
8 In this roofless biome, plants are cultivated in Cornwall's temperate climate. Native Cornish flora is found alongside plants from Australasia and Chile.

Bulb Mania
10 The spring Bulb Mania Festival sees Eden at its most dazzling, when around a million bulbs, including tulips and daffodils, burst into life.

The Core
9 The message of the Eden Project – mankind's dependence on earth's resources – is presented with flair at the Core, an education centre and exhibition venue. The building's design mimics that of a tree. Its centrepiece is *Seed (left)*, a granite sculpture by artist Peter Randall-Page.

Eden – Facts and Figures

Nearly 60 m (200 ft) deep, the former china clay pit required 85,000 tonnes of soil (a mix of china clay and composted waste) to transform it into a horticultural wonderland. The site contains over a million plants of more than 5,000 species. Based on designs by architect R B Fuller, Eden's covered biomes are the world's largest conservatories – the 50-m (164-ft) high Rainforest Biome can hold the Tower of London.

Between November and April, the Arena is iced over to provide a spectacular skating rink, with an under-18 ice disco on Thu nights.

Dartmoor

Southern England's greatest expanse of wilderness holds a unique fascination, its heather-strewn slopes and rocky tors haunted by legends and scattered with relics of the people who inhabited it 3,000 years ago. Hemmed in by the moorland are some of Devon's grandest mansions, its comeliest villages and its most enticing pubs. The main towns of Okehampton and Tavistock hold markets and museums, while Princetown, at the dead centre of the moor, has the main information facilities, which can advise you about organized walks on a network of footpaths that give access to the remotest areas. There is also plenty of scope for cycling and riding, and more adventurous pursuits such as caving, canoeing, climbing and nature safaris.

The Dartmoor Inn

In Lydford, the Castle Inn provides food and drink for the more refined fare of the Dartmoor Inn, *(see p81).*

- Map J4
- Okehampton Castle: Glendale Rd, Okehampton; 01837 52844; adm £3, child £1.50; www.english-heritage.org.uk
- Castle Drogo: Drewsteignton; 01647 433306; castle: adm £7.09, child £3.54, family £17.72; grounds £4.54, child £2.50
- Museum of Dartmoor Life: 3 West St, Okehampton; 01837 52295; open Apr–Oct: 10:15am–4:30pm Mon–Sat; adm £3; www.museumofdartmoorlife.eclipse.co.uk
- Lydford Gorge: The Stables, Lydford; 01822 820320; in winter access restricted to main waterfall & top of gorge; adm £4.85, child £2.40, family £12.15

Top 10 Features

1. Okehampton Castle
2. Castle Drogo
3. Grimspound
4. Museum of Dartmoor Life
5. Dartmeet
6. Widecombe-in-the-Moor
7. Fingle Bridge
8. Lydford Gorge
9. Merrivale Rows
10. Wistman's Wood

Okehampton Castle
A tall, seemingly tottering tower greets you as you approach this ancient Norman construction *(above)* surrounded by woodland. Inside, you can view the remains of the gatehouse, keep and Great Hall.

Castle Drogo
Said to be the last castle in England, this formidable castle was built in the early 20th century by architect Edwin Lutyens on the whim of grocery magnate Julius Drewe. The lush grounds lead down to the River Teign.

Grimspound
To the north of Widecombe, these circular prehistoric huts surrounded by a thick wall *(left)* are said to have been the model for the Stone Age village where Sherlock Holmes camped in the novel, *The Hound of the Baskervilles.*

Call the sights listed in the panel on the left to check opening times.

Museum of Dartmoor Life
This museum *(above)* provides a fascinating insight into lives of the moor's inhabitants, past and present. Displays include everything from antique agricultural tools and farm pick-ups to domestic bric-a-brac.

Dartmeet
This is a renowned beauty spot at the junction of the East and West Dart rivers. Nearby is one of Dartmoor's famous clapper bridges *(centre)* – ancient crossing points.

Widecombe-in-the-Moor
This idyllic village is known for its pinnacled church tower *(above)* – a prominent landmark – and for the famous folk ditty, *Widdicombe Fair*.

Fingle Bridge
Crowds home in on this bridge over the River Teign, but you can find peace on the paths that weave along the shaded banks. The Fingle Bridge Inn provides snacks.

Lydford Gorge
In this remote ravine, the River Lyd tumbles over the 30-m (100-ft) White Lady Waterfall *(above)* and through dense vegetation that shelters wildlife.

Merrivale Rows
Trailing across moorland west of Princetown, these stones give an idea of the kind of prehistoric society that lived here. The complex includes huts and granite tombs.

Wistman's Wood
A couple of miles from the road near Two Bridges, this tangled wood is a remnant of the time when the moor was fully forested. The ancient, mossy trunks creates a fine setting for a picnic.

The Hound of the Baskervilles

This Conan Doyle yarn may have had various possible sources. Local myths tell of a huntsman who terrorized the countryside accompanied by a pack of red-eyed hounds. Another inspiration may have been the legend of the Black Dog of Dartmoor who, it is said, chased late-night travellers on the coach road all the way to their destination.

⁝10 Plymouth

Devon's largest conurbation, and one of Britain's greatest seafaring cities, Plymouth produced such seadogs as Francis Drake and John Hawkins, both of whom played a leading role in the rout of the Spanish Armada in 1588. An important naval base, the city endured ferocious bombing in World War II and fared little better from insensitive rebuilding in the war's aftermath. Fortunately, its historic Barbican district and adjacent harbour have survived intact, along with a handful of timber-framed and jettied historic buildings. Added to these are some compelling modern attractions and a lively cultural scene, all of which repay a visit to this old harbour town.

Monuments on the Hoe

🍴 At the top of Black Friars Distillery, the Barbican Kitchen is perfect for a snack.

• National Marine Aquarium: map Q6; Coxside; 01752 600301; adm £11
• Saltram: map N5; Plympton; 01752 333500; adm £8, garden adm £4
• Mount Edgcumbe: Cremyll, Torpoint; 01752 822236; adm £5
• City Museum and Art Gallery: map Q4; Drake Circus; 01752 304774; adm free
• Crownhill Fort: Crownhill Fort Rd; 01752 793754; adm free
• Merchant's House Museum: map P5; 33 St Andrew's St; 01752 304774; adm £1.50
• Black Friars Distillery: map P5; 60 Southside St; 01752 665292; adm £6
• Elizabethan House: map Q5; 32 New St; 01752 304774; adm £1.50

Top 10 Features

1. Plymouth Hoe
2. National Marine Aquarium
3. Saltram
4. Mount Edgcumbe
5. City Museum and Art Gallery
6. Crownhill Fort
7. Merchant's House Museum
8. Black Friars Distillery
9. Sutton Harbour
10. Elizabethan House

Plymouth Hoe

High above the harbour looking out over Plymouth Sound, the Hoe is a grassy expanse studded with memorials and a relocated lighthouse – Smeaton's Tower *(centre)*. Lawns and flowerbeds make this an ideal spot in fine weather.

National Marine Aquarium

Plymouth's most high-profile attraction *(below)* features a range of marine life, such as sharks, moray eels and seahorses. Panels provide insights into life underwater. Feeding times take place through the day.

Saltram

A Georgian mansion set in its own grounds outside Plymouth, Saltram is adorned with exquisite furnishings *(above)* and works of art. Several films, including *Sense and Sensibility*, have been shot here.

Plymouth Tourist Office: map Q5; Plymouth Mayflower
3–5 The Barbican; 01752 306330; www.plymouth.gov.uk

4 Mount Edgcumbe

Set on the Rame Peninsula facing Plymouth across the Sound, Mount Edgcumbe *(above)* is surrounded by parkland that offers stupendous views of the city and along the coast.

5 City Museum and Art Gallery

The wide-ranging exhibits here include Egyptian statuettes, oriental porcelain, African beadwork and local archaeological finds.

6 Crownhill Fort

Plymouth's finest example of military architecture dates from 1872. It was one of the "Palmerston forts", built to defend the country from a French invasion.

7 Merchant's House Museum

This 17th-century building *(above)* houses a collection of curiosities including a ducking stool, a Victorian doll's house, a pharmacy and a reconstructed schoolroom.

8 Black Friars Distillery

Originally a merchant's house, this distillery has been producing Plymouth Gin since 1793. It is believed that the Pilgrim Fathers *(see p34)* sought shelter here before journeying on the *Mayflower*.

9 Sutton Harbour

The harbour *(below)* was the embarkation point for Captain Cook, and, in 1620, for the Pilgrim Fathers as marked by the Mayflower Steps and a plaque.

10 Elizabethan House

This Tudor home preserves its low ceilings and creaking oak floors. A restored kitchen is on the ground floor, the dining room and parlour on the first floor and bedrooms on the second.

The Historical Port

Formerly a small fishing community, Plymouth prospered in the 15th and 16th centuries as a naval base and a port for wool shipments. The Pilgrim Fathers embarked from here in 1620 to found the American colony of New Plymouth. Captain Cook and Charles Darwin both sailed from here in later centuries. The city's naval presence continues to be strong.

Call the sights to check opening times and tours.

Left **The Citadel** Centre **Bowling Green Hotel** Right **Memorial to the Spanish Armada**

🔟 The Plymouth Hoe

Drake's Statue
This statue of Drake gazes grandly over the Sound. His cutlass and globe represent his circumnavigation of the world. 🗺 *Map P6*

Smeaton's Tower
Originally built in 1759 on Eddystone Rocks miles out to sea, the top half of this lighthouse was rebuilt on the Hoe in 1882. A popular attraction, it affords lofty sea views. 🗺 *Map P6 • 01752 304774 • Open Apr–Sep: 10am–noon, 1–4:30pm Tue–Fri, closes 4pm Sat; Oct–Mar: 10am–noon, 1–3pm Tue–Sat • Adm • www.plymouth.gov.uk*

Smeaton's Tower

Naval Memorial
This obelisk commemorates more than 23,000 dead and missing sailors from Plymouth and other Commonwealth nations in the two world wars. 🗺 *Map P6*

The waterfront at the Hoe

Tinside Lido
This elegant outdoor pool is located right next to the sea and below the Hoe. It is the perfect place for lounging and relaxing. Built in 1935, it is not heated, but the sheer Art Deco exuberance compensates for any chill. 🗺 *Map P6 • Hoe Road • 08703 000042 • Open late May–late Jul: noon–6pm Mon–Fri, 10am–6pm Sat & Sun; late Jul–early Sep: 10am–6pm daily except 7:30pm Wed • www.plymouth.gov.uk*

City of Plymouth Bowling Club
Sir Francis Drake is believed to have insisted on finishing his game of bowls at this club on the Hoe before sailing to meet the Spanish Armada. 🗺 *Map P6 • Lockyer Street • Open late Apr–Sep • 01752 339920*

The Promenade
Enjoy the distant views, tidy lawns and the pretty flowerbeds from this broad promenade running across the Hoe. 🗺 *Map P6*

Royal Citadel
Towering over the quayside at the base of the Hoe, this sturdy fortress was built in 1666 and is

Top 10 Events in Drake's Life

1 Born in Tavistock, Dartmoor, around 1540.

2 Apprenticed to a coastal vessel around 1553.

3 Enlists in the fleet of the Hawkins family in 1563.

4 In 1572, becomes the first Englishman to sight the Pacific.

5 Drake is the first Englishman to circumnavigate the world, 1577–80. Knighted by Queen Elizabeth.

6 Becomes Mayor of Plymouth, 1581. Moves into Buckland Abbey.

7 Plunders Spain's American possessions in command of a fleet of 25 ships in 1585.

8 Drake raids Cadiz and delays the Spanish invasion fleet of Philip II by a year.

9 Plays a leading part in defeating the Spanish Armada in 1588.

10 Drake dies of fever in West Indies in 1596.

Sir Francis Drake

The most renowned seaman of the Elizabethan Age and one of the world's greatest sailors, Francis Drake won fame and fortune on his raids against the Spanish Main. With his exploits, not least his circumnavigation of the globe and his subsequent role in defeating the Spanish Armada, he embodied many of the virtues of expansionist Elizabethan England. He achieved official recognition when he was knighted by the Queen. Though he also participated in the slave trade, his seamanship and military skill made him a national hero.

A statue of Sir Francis Drake

still a military base. Visitors can tour the ramparts, St Katherine's Chapel and the Governor's House. ◈ *Map P6–Q6* • *Guided tours: open May–Sep 2:30pm Tue & Thu* • *Adm*

8 Memorial to the Spanish Armada

This memorial dates from 1890 and is surmounted by a bronze figure of Britannia. The shields on the base show the arms of the towns that contributed men, money and ships to the English fleet. ◈ *Map P6*

9 Air Force Memorial

Topped by a bare-headed pilot, this memorial records the huge losses suffered by the Royal Air Force in World War II, mostly from Bomber Command. Commonwealth and Allied losses are also remembered. ◈ *Map N6*

10 The View

The magnificent panorama from the Hoe extends over Plymouth Sound – the sheltered estuary basin – embracing Drake's Island, the breakwater and usually a flotilla of sailing vessels. ◈ *Map P6–N6*

Devon and Cornwall's Top 10

TOP 10 Exeter

Rising up from the River Exe and dominated by the twin towers of its cathedral, Exeter holds more historical interest than any other city in the region. The days when it was a byword for provincial respectability are long past and Exeter now has a vibrant cultural life, enlivened by students from its university and a range of festivals and live performances that are held throughout the year. Its compact centre is easy to negotiate on foot, while the Quay is a pleasant spot to sit and have a snack. In the evening, pick from its many restaurants or visit one of the city's historic pubs.

Prospect Inn

🍴 **Eat at outdoor tables at the 17th-century Prospect Inn on the quay.**

• Tourist office: map Q2; Dix's Field, Paris St; 01392 665700; www.exeter.gov.uk
• Exeter Cathedral: map Q2; Cathedral Close; 01392 285983; open 9:50am–5pm; adm £4, students & senior citizens £2; www.exeter-cathedral.org.uk
• The Guildhall: map P2; High St; 01392 665500
• Bill Douglas Centre: map P2; University of Exeter, The Old Library, Prince of Wales Rd; 01392 264321; www.billdouglas.org
• Underground Passages: map Q2; 2 Paris St; 01392 665887; adm £5, child (5–18) £3.50
• St Nicholas Priory: map P2; The Mint, off Fore St; 01392 665858; adm £2; www.exeter.gov.uk
• Exeter Phoenix: map P2; Gandy Street; 01392 667080; www.exeterphoenix.org.uk

Top 10 Features

1. Exeter Cathedral
2. The Quay
3. Stepcote Hill
4. The Guildhall
5. Bill Douglas Centre
6. Underground Passages
7. St Nicholas Priory
8. Along the Exe
9. Quay House
10. Exeter Phoenix

Exeter Cathedral

Sheltered within the harmonious Close, the cathedral's most compelling features lie in its 14th-century Gothic style, notably its carved, honey-coloured façade *(centre)* and its vaulted nave – the longest in the country.

The Quay

Once a hard-working harbour, the Quay *(above)* now offers peace and quiet by day, with only a few cafés, craft and antique shops. In contrast, the evenings can be lively, with pubs and clubs drawing in the crowds.

Stepcote Hill

This steep, medieval lane was once a busy main route into town. Tudor buildings *(below)* stand at the bottom alongside one of Exeter's oldest churches, St Mary Steps.

For opening times and other information, call the sights or check their websites.

The Guildhall

Dating from 1330, this building *(above)* still serves municipal functions but you can pop in to admire the portraits in the main chamber.

Bill Douglas Centre

Cinematic memorabilia is displayed in this centre located on the university campus. Exhibits range from early movie cameras and Charlie Chaplin posters to Shirley Temple dolls and *E.T.* money boxes.

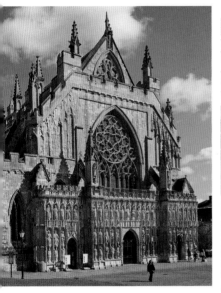

Underground Passages

This subterranean network was built in the 14th century to carry water into the city. Guided tours through the tunnels are fascinating.

St Nicholas Priory

This Benedictine priory survived the Dissolution of the Monasteries. Medieval household objects *(above)* are displayed on the first floor.

Along the Exe

Enjoy a tranquil walk or cycle ride along the Exeter Ship Canal and the Exe Estuary, and spot a range of birdlife along the way. Bikes can be hired from the Quay.

Quay House

This restored 17th-century building on the quay now houses a visitor centre with an audiovisual exhibition of the city's history, as well as models and paintings.

Exeter Phoenix

At the forefront of the local arts scene, this media centre comprises three galleries, a cinema *(right)* and a performance venue. Events of the Vibraphonic music festival are staged here every March.

Exeter's Festivals

The biggest arts festivals are the Summer Festival in late June and the Autumn Festival in November, featuring dance, comedy and music. Vibraphonic in March concentrates solely on music, while local gastronomy is celebrated at the Food and Drink Festival (March/April), which includes cookery demonstrations and hands-on activities for kids.

Left **Buildings on Cathedral Close** Right **Stained-glass windows adorning the cathedral**

🔟 Exeter Cathedral

Gothic Façade
Apostles, prophets and soldiers jostle for space on the crowded carved West Front of the cathedral. Also look out for the kings Alfred, Athelstan, Canute, William I and Richard II.

Ceiling
This is the longest unbroken Gothic ceiling in the world. It makes an immediate impression with a dense network of rib-vaulting, shafts and mouldings. One of the ceiling bosses shows the murder of Thomas à Becket, Archbishop of Canterbury, in 1170.

Minstrels' Gallery
High up on the left side of the nave is a minstrels' gallery, which was built in 1350. It depicts 12 angels playing musical instruments.

Sepulchre of Hugh Courtenay
The cathedral is crammed with tombs, none more eye-catching than the 14th-century sepulchres of Hugh Courtenay, earl of Devon, and his wife. Their tomb is carved with graceful swans and a lion.

Chapter House
From the right transept, a door leads into the Chapter House, originally constructed in the 1220s but mostly rebuilt after a fire in 1413. Beneath the fine timber ceiling stands an array of sculptures from the 20th century. The Chapter House is also a venue for classical concerts. You can pick up a leaflet for details.

The Exeter Clock

Exeter Clock
The clock in the left transept dates from the late-15th century, though the minutes dial was added only in 1759. The sun and moon revolve round the earth, in the form of a golden ball.

Choir
Dominated by a 18-m (60-ft) bishop's throne and a massive organ case, the Choir (or "Quire") holds stalls dating from the 19th century, but with carvings that date from as far back as the 1250s, one showing an elephant.

The Minstrels' Gallery

Top 10 Key Events in Exeter's History

1. Exeter is fortified by the Romans in AD 50–55.
2. Around 878, the city is re-founded by Alfred the Great.
3. In 1068, the Normans take control and expand the wool trade.
4. The countess of Devon diverts the shipping trade to Topsham in the late-13th century.
5. In 1369, work is completed on the Exeter Cathedral.
6. In 1564–66, the Quay and the Ship Canal are constructed.
7. The city shelters Charles I's queen in 1643, but falls to the Roundheads in 1646.
8. Trade ceases during the Napoleonic wars (1800–15), damaging the local textile industry.
9. World War II bombing flattens the city centre.
10. In 2007, the Princesshay development spearheads a regeneration of the historic centre.

Cannon outside Custom House on the Quay

Exeter's History

Previously a settlement of the Celtic Dumnonii tribe, Exeter became the most westerly outpost of the Roman Empire in Britain when it was garrisoned in around AD 50–55. Saxon settlement was followed by Danish attacks, but conditions were peaceful under the Norman regime after 1068. Its position on the River Exe allowed it to become a major outlet for wool shipments. During the Civil War, Exeter became the western headquarters of the Royalists and sheltered Charles I's queen. In the 20th century, bombing during World War II spared the cathedral, but devastated the historic centre. However, the founding of the University of Exeter in 1955 has helped inject new energy into the city, and the new Princesshay development has reversed some of the damage done by shabby post-war reconstruction.

8 Plaque to R D Blackmore

Among the tombs and memorials that line the walls of the aisles is one near the door, which is dedicated to R D Blackmore *(see p56)*, author of the rip-roaring Exmoor tale, *Lorna Doone*.

9 Cathedral Close

The lawns surrounding the cathedral are a pleasant place to relax. They are over-looked by an array of historical buildings, including the splendid Elizabethan Mol's Coffee House, which is now a boutique. The remains of a Roman bath house and a Saxon burial site lie beneath the lawns.

10 The Towers

Dating from the 12th century, the two central towers are the oldest part of the cathedral. They are still the most conspicuous feature of Exeter's skyline.

Tresco Abbey Gardens

Like a cross between Kew Gardens and the Amazonian jungle, Tresco Abbey Gardens is a botanical wonderland, with feathery ferns, tall palms and spreading succulents. The sheltered conditions on Tresco, aided by wind- and salt-tolerant Monterey pines and cypresses, have created a sympathetic home for this oasis of some 20,000 plants from 80 countries. These range from spider plants to brilliant flame trees, aromatic myrtle and yellow-flowering acacias. The gardens are scarcely less exuberant in winter when over 60 aloe plants, as well as yuccas from Mexico and Australian banksias, are in full bloom.

Top 10 Features

1. The Plants
2. Valhalla
3. Visitor Centre
4. The Abbey Buildings
5. The Mediterranean Garden
6. The Long Walk
7. The Top Terrace
8. Statuary
9. Magnificent Views
10. Neptune Steps

Exotic plants in bloom

🔵 For a quiet break from the gardens, head down to nearby Appletree Bay, one of the island's best beaches.

🟢 If you don't want to stop in the Gardens' café, try Tresco's New Inn *(see p102)* for tasty bar meals and good beer.

• Map A4
• Tresco, Isles of Scilly, Cornwall
• 01720 424105
• www.tresco.co.uk
• Open 10am–4pm daily
• Adm £9, children under 16 free

The Plants
Visiting Tresco's gardens *(centre)* is like making a horticultural world tour. You will see flowered echiums from the Canary Islands, silver trees from South Africa, wine palms from Chile and spiky *agaves* from Mexico.

Valhalla
This exhibition of figure-heads *(above)* and pieces recovered from shipwrecks around the islands makes an interesting sideshow. The collection, started by Augustus Smith, is named after the mythological Norse palace where the souls of slain heroes feast eternally.

Visitor Centre
Built with trees felled by winter gales, the visitor centre serves teas and lunches, and also has a shop that sells garden guides, seeds and plants.

The Abbey Buildings
The remains of St Nicholas Priory form a harmonious backdrop to the fine foliage. The abbey's archway *(above)* is today an iconic image of Tresco's gardens.

5 The Mediterranean Garden

From the entrance, a startling blue wooden bridge *(above)* leads visitors to the Mediterranean Garden, with a shell house and a fountain at its centre.

6 The Long Walk

Running the length of the gardens, the shaded Long Walk has ferns and Nikau Palms from New Zealand, and large, mature trees such as the Tasmanian Blue Gum with its multiple stems.

7 The Top Terrace

The highest terrace of the gardens is warmer and drier than other parts and hosts plants from Australia and South Africa. Its eastern end overlooks the old Abbey.

8 Statuary

Scattered across the site are exotic statues and sculptures, such as the serenely smiling earth mother *Gaia* *(above)* next to the Neptune Steps, by sculptor David Wynne.

9 Magnificent Views

Tantalizing glimpses of the ocean *(below)* and neighbouring islands are all around. The best vistas are from Abbey Hill, Olive Terrace in the Mediterranean Garden, and the Top Terrace.

10 Neptune Steps

The granite-carved steps are flanked by clay pots designed by the garden's creator, Augustus Smith, and topped by a giant figure of Neptune, which was once a ship's figurehead.

Emperor of Scilly

Tresco Gardens were founded by Augustus Smith, a key figure in the history of the archipelago, who took over the lease for the islands in 1834. Known as "Emperor Smith of Scilly", he laid the first beds among the abbey ruins after settling on the island. Four generations of his family, up to Robert and Lucy Dorrien-Smith who now run the estate, have continued his work.

🔟 Porthcurno and the Minack Theatre

One of Cornwall's brightest gems is lovely Porthcurno Bay, cupped between cliffs on the southern coast of the Penwith peninsula. Though the village itself is low-key, there are enough attractions in the area to merit a visit. The most unique sight is the famous open-air Minack Theatre, a magical place to take in some culture and entertainment. Below, the wedge of perfect sandy beach provides plenty of amusement by day, while the coast path to either side runs through a majestic landscape that is managed by the National Trust. Smaller beaches and a scattering of historical relics lie within a short clamber.

Minack Coffee Shop

🚫 The beach and theatre are not suitable for anyone with mobility problems.

🍴 Snacks are available at the Minack Coffee Shop; alternatively try the Porthcurno Beach Café for baguettes and flapjacks (01736 810834).

• Map A6
• Minack Theatre and Exhibition Centre: Porthcurno, Cornwall; 01736 810694
• Exhibition Centre: adm £3.50 adults, child £1.40, senior citizens £2.50
• Minack Box Office: 01736 810181; tickets adm £7–£8.50, under-16 £3.50–£4.50; www.minack.com
• Porthcurno Telegraph Museum: Porthcurno, Cornwall; 01736 810966; adm £5 adults, child £2.75, concession £4.40, students £3.50, family £12; www.porthcurno.org.uk

Top 10 Features

1. Logan's Rock
2. The View from the Minack
3. The Minack's Rockeries and Gardens
4. Minack Theatre Exhibition Centre
5. Minack Theatre
6. Minack Coffee Shop
7. Porthcurno Telegraph Museum
8. Treryn Dinas Iron Age Fort
9. Pednvounder's White Pyramid
10. Porthcurno Beach

Logan's Rock

The 70-tonne Logan's Rock stands on an outcrop on the eastern edge of Porthcurno Bay *(below)*. It was once said to rock on its perch, but in 1824 a band of sailors dislodged it and now it no longer moves.

The View from the Minack

In sunny weather, you could imagine yourself on Italy's precipitous Amalfi coast as you soak in the inspiring view from this cliffside theatre. The jagged headland forms a magnificent backdrop to performances.

The Minack's Rockeries and Gardens

The rockeries and gardens surrounding the theatre have become an attraction in their own right. The choice of plants – colourful succulents and hardy shrubs *(below)* – is based on plans by Rowena Cade, the Minack's founder.

Minack Theatre Exhibition Centre

This exhibition centre *(above)* tells the remarkable story of the creation of the Minack, which was the inspiration of Rowena Cade in the 1930s.

Minack Theatre

On the cliffs above Porthcurno stands Cornwall's most famous theatre – an amphitheatre set into the rock. Over 17 weeks in summer, you can attend a variety of theatrical performances.

Minack Coffee Shop

There is no more panoramic spot within miles for a snack than this coffee shop, perched on the cliff edge. It is open only to visitors to the Exhibition Centre and play-goers.

Porthcurno Telegraph Museum

In 1870, an undersea cable was laid to North America from Porthcurno. A museum exploring the history of the telegraph system now occupies the terminus, set within a network of tunnels.

Treryn Dinas Iron Age Fort

Logan's Rock forms part of an Iron Age promontory fort. The few traces that can still be seen include four ramparts, and the remains of stone houses within a ditch across the promontory.

Pednvounder's White Pyramid

Halfway along the path to Logan's Rock you will come across this peculiar structure *(below)*, placed here in the 1950s to mark the termination of a telegraph cable, which once crossed the English Channel to France.

Porthcurno Beach

Below the museum, Porthcurno's beach *(above)* is among the finest on the Penwith peninsula. Sheltered by cliffs on either side, the white sand is mixed with tiny shell fragments. Coastal paths lead to Porth Chapel and Pednvounder beaches.

The Building of the Minack

Rowena Cade purchased the Minack headland for £100. She built a house here and began organizing amateur theatre productions for friends in the 1920s. From this developed the more ambitious idea of an open-air theatre and in 1932 the first production was staged – *The Tempest*. Rowena Cade continued to improve the site until her death in 1983.

TOP 10 St Ives

The port and resort of St Ives is like nowhere else in Britain. Its intricate mesh of lanes – bearing such names as Salubrious Place and Teetotal Street – backs onto a bustling quayside and a quartet of sandy beaches, presenting fetching vistas at every turn. Overlooking one beach is the region's premier art gallery, the Tate St Ives, but there are few streets without a scattering of smaller galleries displaying a range of local landscapes and harbour scenes that recall the town's past and its continuing role as a hive of creativity. Added to these is a dense concentration of restaurants and bars, swish hotels and cosy B&Bs squeezed into tiny, flower-bedecked fishermen's cottages.

A café, Porthmeor Beach

🚗 St Ives is a driver's nightmare. Though often full, the most central car parks are Barnoon, above the Tate, or at the station.

🍴 The Tate's rooftop café is ideal for a snack while you take in the panorama.

• Map B5
• Tourist information: Street an Pol; 01736 796297; www.visit-westcornwall.co.uk
• Tate St Ives: Porthmeor Beach; 01736 796226
• St Ives Society of Artists Gallery: Norway Square; 01736 795582
• St Ia: Market Place; 01736 796404
• St Ives Museum, Wheal Dream; 01736 796005
• Leach Pottery: Higher Stennack; 01736 799703
• Barbara Hepworth Museum: Barnoon Hill; 01736 796226; open Mar–Oct 10am–5pm daily; Nov–Feb 10am–5:20pm Tue–Sun

Top 10 Features

1. Tate St Ives
2. St Ives Society of Artists Gallery
3. Porthminster Beach
4. St Ia
5. St Ives Museum
6. St Ives September Festival
7. Trewyn Subtropical Gardens
8. Leach Pottery
9. Porthmeor Beach
10. Barbara Hepworth Museum and Sculpture Garden

1 Tate St Ives
Few British galleries have such a striking setting as this, overlooking a beach. Its circular entrance recalls the gasworks that formerly stood here. The interior is perfect to display local art *(above)*.

2 St Ives Society of Artists Gallery
Housed in the former Mariners Church, this gallery is a good place to take in contemporary work by the Society's members. The Mariners Gallery in the ex-crypt also holds private exhibitions.

3 Porthminster Beach
The largest of St Ives' beaches *(below)* always has space for swimming or lounging and is popular with sand sculptors. The famous Porthminster Beach Café is located here *(see p103)*.

➡ *Call the museums and galleries for opening times and admission fees.*

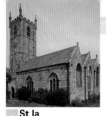

St Ia
4 This 15th-century parish church *(above)* is dedicated to St Ia, the missionary after whom the town is probably named. It has a wagon roof and a granite font.

St Ives Museum
5 Unearthing this museum in the maze of back streets is like discovering a treasure chest of curiosities. The quirky collection covers every aspect of local history, from geology and archaeology to mining, fishing, farming and shipwrecks.

St Ives September Festival
6 This boisterous, 15-day festival features comedy, tribute bands, local folk music and African dance. There is also free music spilling from many pubs.

Trewyn Subtropical Gardens
7 In the heart of St Ives, this quiet retreat *(above)* with banana trees and other subtropical plants is a peaceful spot even in high season, and makes for an ideal picnic venue.

Leach Pottery
8 Britain's foremost potter, Bernard Leach (1887–1979), established this pottery in 1920 to create his Japanese-inspired work *(right)*. Today, you can see exhibitions of his work and watch contemporary ceramicists at work.

Porthmeor Beach
9 Backed by cafés and the façade of the Tate gallery, and with the promontory of the island at its eastern end, Porthmeor *(centre)* is the most accessible beach in St Ives. Its firm sand is ideal for castle-building and beach gear can be rented.

Barbara Hepworth Museum and Sculpture Garden
10 Sculptor Barbara Hepworth was at the core of the mid-20th-century arts scene in St Ives. Her studio is now one of Cornwall's most compelling galleries, displaying her mainly abstract works. Larger pieces are arranged around the lush garden (see p97).

Art in St Ives
Sometime in 1920, potters Bernard Leach and Shoji Hamada settled in St Ives to set up Leach Pottery. A stream of artists followed, including sculptor Barbara Hepworth and painter Ben Nicholson in 1939. Along with later arrivals such as Patrick Heron and Terry Frost, they specialized in abstract works strongly influenced by the Cornish landscape.

🔟 Penzance and St Michael's Mount

The port of Penzance sits in the northern end of Mount's Bay. Georgian buildings characterize much of the town, though its harbourside pool is strictly Art Deco. The town has two excellent galleries that continue in the tradition of the colony of artists who settled in neighbouring Newlyn. Across Mount's Bay, St Michael's Mount (centre) makes an eye-catching sight. Originally a priory dedicated to the Archangel St Michael and marking the southern end of a pilgrim's route, St Michael's Way, the structure was later fortified. Visitors who brave the steep climb to the house are rewarded by stunning views.

Market Jew Street
Penzance's main street *(above)* derives its name from the Cornish "Marghas Yow" which means Thursday Market. The domed Market House is at its very top.

The Admiral Benbow Inn

🕘 The terraced and walled gardens are worth a wander and offer excellent views.

- Map B5
- Tourist office: Station Approach, Penzance; 01736 362207
- Jubilee Pool: The Promenade; 01736 369224; www. jubileepool.co.uk
- The Exchange: Princess St, Penzance; 01736 363715; free;
- Newlyn Art Gallery: New Rd, Newlyn; 01736 363715; free; www. newlynartgallery.co.uk
- Penlee House: Morrab Rd, Penzance; 01736 363625; adm £3, free Sat; www.penleehouse. org.uk
- St Michael's Mount: Marazion; 01736 710507; castle: adm £6.60, family £16.50; garden: adm £3; child £1, ferry £1.50; www. stmichaelsmount.co.uk

Top 10 Features

1. Market Jew Street
2. Chapel Street
3. Jubilee Pool
4. The Exchange
5. Newlyn
6. Penlee House
7. The Causeway, St Michael's Mount
8. The Blue Drawing Room, St Michael's Mount
9. The Chapel, St Michael's Mount
10. The Chevy Chase Room, St Michael's Mount

Chapel Street
Handsome Chapel Street has some of Penzance's comeliest buildings, including the flamboyant Egyptian House *(above)*, dating from 1830. Across the road is the Union Hotel which features a minstrels' gallery.

Jubilee Pool
Off Penzance's harbour, this open-air lido was opened in 1935, the year of George V's silver jubilee. It is spacious and sleek, and has a safe children's area.

The Exchange
Behind an impressive glass façade, the ground floor of the town's old telephone exchange boasts the largest single exhibition space within 300 km (180 miles).

Call the sights to check opening times.

Newlyn
To the south of Penzance and at a walkable distance, Newlyn is a busy fishing port *(above)* with a thriving early-morning fish market. Attractions include the Newlyn Art Gallery, which showcases contemporary art.

Penlee House
The Newlyn school of artists who settled in the area in the late 19th century *(see p35)* are well-represented in this Victorian gallery and museum set within a park. The exhibits reflect the town's fishing and mining heritage.

The Causeway, St Michael's Mount
Off the Marazion coast, the promontory on which St Michael's Mount stands can be reached by boat, but at low tide, you can walk across on a causeway *(below)*.

The Blue Drawing Room, St Michael's Mount
This exquisite room in a Rococo style has furnishings in a delightful Wedgewood Blue.

The Chapel, St Michael's Mount
A door from the Blue Drawing Room leads into the Priory Church, at the summit of the island. The church is still regularly used for services. The walls are lined with memorials to the St Aubyn family, who have held the castle since 1659.

The Chevy Chase Room, St Michael's Mount
This room is named after its 17th-century plaster frieze depicting hunting scenes described in the *Ballad of Chevy Chase*. A Jacobean oak table *(left)* dominates the room.

St Michael's Mount – History and Legend
Built as a Benedictine priory in 1135 by the Abbot of Mont St Michel in Normandy, St Michael's Mount was granted to Colonel John St Aubyn after the civil war. His descendants have held it ever since. However, legend has it that the mount was the lair of Comoran the giant, who came ashore to steal sheep and was killed by a boy, Jack.

Visiting St Michael's Mount is unsuitable for people with mobility problems.

🔟 Padstow

Tucked into the Camel Estuary, Padstow is one of Cornwall's most attractive ports. Lively and smart, the town is well-placed for beaches, with some of the county's best – Daymer, Polzeath, Trevone, Constantine – within a short distance. This is mainly a fishing port whose catch is taken daily to auctions at Brixham and Newlyn, though plenty also ends up in local eateries. Foodies will know the town primarily as the domain of celebrity seafood chef Rick Stein, who has raised Padstow's profile with his luxury hotels and seafood restaurants, which are among the best in the country. Such is his grip on the place that it has been nicknamed "Padstein".

Rick Stein's Café

🔗 Enquire at the tourist office about open-air brass band concerts, performed on most Sundays and some weekdays in summer.

• Map D3
• Tourist information: North Quay; 01841 533449
• Rick Stein's restaurants: see p87 (Rick Stein's Café; St Petroc's Bistro; Seafood Restaurant; Stein's Fish & Chips)
• Prideaux Place: 01841 532411; open Apr & early May–early Oct: 1:30–5pm Sun–Thu, last tour 4pm; adm £7.50. grounds £2; www. prideauxplace.co.uk
• Padstow Museum: Market Place; 01841 532752; open Apr–Oct: 10:30am–4:30pm Mon–Fri, 10:30am–1:30pm Sat
• St Petroc's Church: Church St; 01841 533776
• National Lobster Hatchery: South Quay; 01841 533877; open 10am daily, closing times vary

Top 10 Features

1. Padstow Harbour
2. The Camel Trail
3. Rick Stein's Restaurants
4. The Camel Estuary
5. Prideaux Place
6. Padstow Museum
7. Obby Oss
8. The Saints' Way
9. St Petroc's Church
10. The National Lobster Hatchery

1 Padstow Harbour

The town's inner harbour *(right)* is where crowds gather to see the catch being brought in. On the quayside is Abbey House, Padstow's oldest building. Explore the estuary on boat trips.

2 The Camel Trail

This is Cornwall's finest walking and cycling route *(below)*. It follows the track of an out-of-use railway alongside the River Camel for 34 km (17 miles). You can rent bikes from Padstow and Wadebridge.

3 Rick Stein's Restaurants

Sample delightful seafood at the Seafood Restaurant. The culinary master also runs three hotels, a café, a patisserie and a fish-and-chip takeaway in Padstow.

4 The Camel Estuary

The major river on Cornwall's northern coast, the Camel is a haven for wading migrant birds that feed on the fertile mudflats. It derives its name from the Cornish *cam pol*, or winding river. Passenger ferries cross the estuary from Padstow to Rock.

Prideaux Place

On a hill overlooking the town, this Elizabethan manor house *(above)* has richly furnished rooms and superlative plasterwork. Outside are formal gardens and a deer park. The films *Twelfth Night, Oscar and Lucinda* were shot here.

Padstow Museum

Housed in the Old Institute building, this little museum is crowded with archaeological items, nautical models, old photos and a scary Obby Oss costume.

Obby Oss

One of Cornwall's most flamboyant festivals *(above)* takes place on May 1 or 2. Processions around the town are led by a figure in an outlandish costume *(see p39)*.

The Saints' Way

Crossing the peninsula between Padstow and Fowey, this 45-km (28-mile) trail follows the route taken by pilgrims. It follows ancient footpaths and quiet country lanes. The official starting point in Padstow is St Petroc's Church.

St Petroc's Church

Padstow was once known as Petrocstowe, from the missionary St Petroc, who is said to have crossed the Irish Sea on a cabbage leaf. St Petroc's Church *(above)* is famous for its 15th- or 16th-century front carved from Catacleuse stone.

The National Lobster Hatchery

Get up close to various crustaceans at this fascinating exhibition. The tanks hold creatures such as spider crabs, crayfish and sponges, varying in size from inch-long baby lobsters to the giant old Dai the Claw.

The Obby Oss Tale

The origins of Obby Oss are lost but it includes elements of many other May Day festivities, and is similar to one held in Minehead, Somerset. Controlled by club-wielding "Teazers", the Obby Oss figures, in twirling hooped gowns, are probably intended to drive winter away, while spring is represented by the white-clothed escort. The festivities begin the previous night when the Blue Ribbon Oss emerges from the Golden Lion pub.

Left **Buckfast Abbey** Right **Reconstructed Anglo Saxon village**

Moments in History

1 50–55 AD: Roman Invasion

The Romans occupied Exeter and established a strong garrison here without penetrating further west, where Celtic tribes held sway. The region benefited from the Roman occupation, though few vestiges of that culture remain.

2 6th and 7th Centuries: Anglo-Saxon Settlements

During Roman withdrawal, Saxon tribes began to settle in the region, but made little headway against the Celtic tribes, whose strongholds were concentrated in Cornwall. The Arthurian legends are probably derived from the exploits of one of the Celtic chieftains, who continued to resist the Anglo-Saxons.

3 11th to 16th Centuries: The Wool Industry

Devon's wool industry flourished under the stability imposed by the Normans. Landowners of fertile inland pastures built mansions and merchants exported produce to Europe from the southern ports, which grew rich.

4 1530s: Dissolution of the Monasteries

The great monastic houses, which wielded huge influence and power in Devon and Cornwall, were suppressed by order of Henry VIII. Some, like the Benedictine abbey of Tavistock, were destroyed; others, like Buckfast Abbey, became mansions of wealthy merchants.

5 1558–1603: The Elizabethan Era

Devon became a strategic region during the contest against Spain. Exeter and Plymouth in particular were important military and naval bases. The great western sea-ports benefited from the expansion of transatlantic trade and the first English colonists of the New World set sail from here.

6 1642–51: The Civil War

Most of the region sided with the Royalists during England's Civil War, though both Exeter and Plymouth originally supported the Parliamentarians. Charles I defeated the Earl of Essex's army in 1644 but Royalists were checked by Thomas Fairfax's army. This led to the fall of Pendennis Castle and Exeter in 1646.

7 18th Century: Tin and Copper Mining

Under the Normans, Cornwall had become Europe's biggest source of tin. A series

Statue of John Wesley

Preceding pages **Boats moored at St Ives harbour**

Remains of Wheal Basset tin mine

of scientific advances in the 18th century allowed the tin and copper mining industry to become highly profitable. Copper mining, concentrated around Redruth and Camborne, peaked in the 1840s.

1743–86: Spread of Wesleyism

The impoverished conditions of the region's miners led to widespread acceptance of the Methodist preaching of John Wesley. Methodist chapels are still visible in the region today.

1884 onwards: Artists' Colonies Established

Drawn by intense light, dramatic seascapes and the life of fishing communities, painter Stanhope Forbes settled in Newlyn in 1884 and became the leading figure in the artists' colony. Neighbouring St Ives continues to be an important artistic hub.

1939–45: World War II

Although most of the West Country was designated safe from German attack and received evacuees from London and the Midlands, Plymouth suffered the worst bombing of any British seaport. Exeter was also targeted in the "Baedeker raids", which were aimed at cultural centres mentioned in Baedeker guidebooks.

Top 10 Arthurian Sites

1 Tintagel Castle
The most evocative of all Arthurian sights is believed to be his birthplace (see p83).

2 Slaughterbridge
This spot on Bodmin Moor is said to be the site of King Arthur's last battle, against his nephew Mordred. ◈ Map E3

3 Dozmary Pool
It is said that Arthur's sword Excalibur was thrown here and received by the Lady of the Lake. ◈ Map E3

4 The Tristan Stone
This monument marks the grave of Drustanus, identified with Tristan (or Tristram), one of Arthur's knights. ◈ Map E4

5 Lyonnesse
A fabled land sunk beneath the waves, Lyonnesse is a candidate for Arthur's birthplace. ◈ Map A6

6 Loe Pool
Like Dozmary Pool, this is where Excalibur was believed to be restored to the Lady of the Lake. ◈ Map B6

7 Camelford
This town on Bodmin Moor is one of several places identified with Camelot. ◈ Map E3

8 Castle Dore
An Iron Age hillfort said to have been King Mark of Cornwall's home (see p94).

9 Boscastle
After his last battle, Arthur's body was supposedly transported to this North Cornwall port. ◈ Map D2

10 Castle an Dinas
This important hillfort outside St Columb Major is believed to be Arthur's hunting lodge. ◈ Map D4

Left **A woodland path on the Saints' Way** Right **St Michael's Way**

🔟 Great Walks

1 Hall Walk

One of the best short walks in Cornwall, this 6-km (4-mile) amble explores the area around Fowey. Passing through woods overlooking the harbour and river, the path climbs above Pont Pill – where you may spot herons and curlews – and takes in a memorable panorama from Penleath Point. ✎ *Map E4*

2 Two Moors Way/Coast to Coast Walk

The Two Moors Way which links Exmoor and Dartmoor can be extended at its southern end between Ivybridge and Plymouth to make a 180-km (112-mile) coast-to-coast hike. The most dramatic scenery is on Dartmoor, though Lynmouth at the northern end makes a striking starting or finishing post. ✎ *Map K1*

3 Hobby Drive

Above the chocolate-box village of Clovelly, this shady 5-km (3-mile) stroll affords glorious views over the harbour and Bideford Bay. Spring is the best time, when beech leaves shimmer above carpets of bluebells. ✎ *Map C2*

4 Saints' Way

Cornwall's coast-to-coast trail covers about 48 km (30 miles) between Padstow and Fowey. Though there is no evidence of the whole route being used in the Middle Ages, parts of it were certainly travelled by pilgrims en route to shrines, holy wells and chapels. ✎ *Map D3*

5 Tarka Trail

Inspired by Henry Williamson's animal tale, *Tarka the Otter (see p68)*, this figure-of-eight route centring on Barnstaple takes in coastal and inland areas of North Devon. If you include the section covered by the Tarka Line between Eggesford and Barnstaple, the route is 288 km (180 miles) long *(see p67)*.

Crossing moorland on the Two Moors Way

Dart Valley Trail

6 You can experience the glories of the Dart Valley on this 26-km (16-mile) walk, which swoops high above or runs along-side the River Dart. Half of it is a circuit, involving two ferry cros-sings, and the other half follows the river to Totnes. ◈ *Map J5*

Dartmoor Way

7 For more than 144 km (90 miles), this circular route crosses some of Dartmoor's most thrilling terrain including rugged moor, wooded valleys and disused railway tracks. Much of the trail – like the area bet-ween Tavistock and Okehampton – skirts the edge of the moor, but it also takes in Princetown in the centre of Dartmoor. ◈ *Map J4*

South West Coast Path

8 England's longest National Trail – 1,014 km (630 miles) – is used by anyone who walks for any length along the Devon and Cornwall seaboard. Kicking off in Minehead in Somerset, winding along the indented coasts of Devon, Cornwall and finally Dorset, the trail is predominantly hilly and often dramatic.

East Devon Way

9 Also known as the Foxglove Way, this undulating inland trail follows footpaths, bridleways and lanes between Exmouth and Uplyme, north of Lyme Regis over the Dorset border. It is 61 km (38 miles) long. ◈ *Map L4*

St Michael's Way

10 Weaving a meandering route between Lelant, near St Ives, and Marazion, this 19.5-km (12.5-mile) trail was once used by pilg-rims and travellers to avoid the treacherous waters around Land's End. ◈ *Map B5*

Top 10 Outdoor Activities

Horse-Riding

1 Stables exist all over the region and offer escorted treks for riders of all abilities.

Hiking

2 The simplest (and cheap-est) way to experience the beauty of the region.

Canoeing

3 The rivers of Dartmoor and the great waterways of Cornwall can be enjoyed on a canoe trip.

Coasteering

4 This increasingly popular pursuit involves negotiating rocky coasts using a variety of means.

Sailing

5 Salcombe, Dartmouth, Falmouth and Fowey offer facilities for sailors of all levels.

Surfing

6 Some of Britain's top surfing beaches can be found in the West Country with ann-ual competitions at Newquay.

Windsurfing

7 The region's bays and inlets are ideal for wind-surfers, with rental equipment available at many places.

Diving

8 The wrecks and reefs of Devon and Cornwall draw diving enthusiasts from far and wide.

Gig Racing

9 Ex-pilot boats are raced off the coastal villages of West Cornwall in summer, most famously in the Isles of Scilly.

Sea Safaris

10 Take to the seas on organized whale-, seal- and shark-watching excursions during summer.

Left **Morris dancers at Sidmouth Folk Week** Right **Tar barrelling**

Festivals

Helston's Flora Day
This Cornish extravaganza is truly unique, involving a stately procession of top-hatted people in frocks performing the "Furry Dance" through the streets of Helston. Flowers and sprigs of sycamore are a feature of this spring festival. ◈ *Map B5* • *May 8 (or previous Sat if date falls on Sun or Mon)*

St Ives September Festival
The arts have long had a strong presence in St Ives and this two-week jamboree brings them together with exhibitions, drama and poetry readings. Music ranges from cello recitals to tribute pop acts and African beats, with most performances held in St Ia Church and the Guildhall. There are also talks and comedy acts. ◈ *Map B5* • *Mid-Sep* • *www.stivesseptemberfestival.co.uk*

Daphne du Maurier Festival, Fowey
The author, who lived in Fowey, is celebrated at this 10-day literary festival featuring music,

drama, themed walks through the town and daily talks by well-known personalities. ◈ *Map E4* • *Mid-May* • *www.dumaurierfestival.co.uk*

Sidmouth Folk Week
Folk music, Northumbrian pipes and Morris dancers feature at a seaside festival in one of Devon's most elegant towns. Even non-folk fans succumb to the upbeat charm of the event, with buskers lining the Esplanade and pubs jammed with carousers. Accommodation and concert tickets get snapped up quickly. ◈ *Map L4* • *Early Aug* • *www.sidmouthfolkweek.co.uk*

Tar Barrelling, Ottery St Mary
Every Bonfire Night barrels that have been soaked in tar are set alight and hoisted around town. Each of Ottery's central pubs sponsors a barrel – 17 in all. The evening culminates in fireworks around a huge bonfire beside the River Otter. ◈ *Map L3* • *Nov 5 (or previous Sat if date falls on Sun or Mon)*

Padstow's Obby Oss character

6 Golowan Festival, Penzance

This week-long arts and dance festival features processions, circus performers, buskers and a mock mayoral election. The Golowan Band provides music, while flaming torches and fire-works add to the spectacle. ✪ Map B5 • Late Jun • www.golowan.org

7 Dartmouth Royal Regatta

The three-day regatta highlights the town's nautical traditions with rowing races and yachting displays. It became "Royal" after an unscheduled visit by Queen Victoria in 1856. The festival has a distinct martial flavour with military bands and an exciting air display by the RAF (see p80).

8 Obby Oss, Padstow

Pagan fertility rites and local traditions unite in this May Day spectacle. The main character, the Obby Oss, garbed in a black costume draped around a 2-m (6-ft) wide hoop, is accompanied by a "Teazer" with music, drums and the May Song. ✪ Map D3 • May 1 (or May 2 if date falls on Sun)

9 Oyster Festival, Falmouth

This four-day event pays homage to Cornish seafood. There's music from the local brass band, oyster-shucking competitions, cookery demonstrations and boat races. ✪ Map C5 • Mid-Oct • www.falmouthoysterfestival.co.uk

10 Lowender Peran, Perranporth

Cornwall's Celtic heritage is the theme of this festival, which features music, poetry and acts from Scottish, Irish, Welsh, Manx and Breton performers. ✪ Map C4 • Mid-Oct • www.lowenderperan.co.uk

Top 10 Live Music and Theatre Venues

1 Exeter Phoenix

This arts centre holds the Vibraphonic music festival in March (see p19).

2 Eden Project

This is Cornwall's best outdoor music venue in summer (see pp10–11).

3 The Cavern, Exeter

Bands play nightly at this underground venue. ✪ Map K4 • 83–4 Queen St • 01392 495370 • www.cavernclub.co.uk

4 Hall for Cornwall, Truro

Drama and music are staged here. ✪ Map C5 • Back Quay, Truro • 01872 262466 • www.hallforcornwall.co.uk

5 Exeter Northcott

Exeter's principal theatre venue. ✪ Map K4 • Stocker Rd • 01392 493493 • www.exeternorthcott.co.uk

6 Minack Theatre

This cliff-top amphitheatre hosts a range of productions in summer (see pp24–5).

7 Acorn Arts Centre

This former church is now a playhouse. ✪ Map B5 • Parade St, Penzance • 01736 365520 • www.acornartscentre.co.uk

8 Plymouth Pavilions

A large multi-purpose complex. ✪ Map H5 • Millbay Rd, Plymouth • 08451 461460 • www.plymouthpavilions.com

9 Barbican Theatre

Theatre specializing in new drama. ✪ Map H5 • Castle St, Plymouth • 01752 267131 • www.barbicantheatre.co.uk

10 Theatre Royal

Mainstream shows are held in the main venue; cutting-edge work in the Drum Theatre. ✪ Map H5 • Royal Parade, Plymouth • 01752 267222 • www.theatreroyal.com

Left **Porthcurno Beach** Right **Whitesand Bay**

🔟 Great Beaches

1 Porthcurno
One of the finest bays of the Penwith Peninsula, Porthcurno, with its wedge of white sand mixed with tiny shells, is squeezed between granite cliffs. The rock-hewn Minack Theatre is located to one side and there is a museum of telegraphy at the back of the beach. Pubs and cafés can be found close by *(see pp24–5)*.

2 Par Beach, Isles of Scilly
Majestic, bare and wild, the beaches on St Martin's are considered to be the best on the Isles of Scilly. Par Beach on the island's southern shore is probably the most impressive – a long, empty strand looking out onto rocks that make up the Eastern Isles. Be prepared for chilly water though. ◈ *Map B4*

3 Whitesand Bay
This expanse of fine sand close to Land's End is a favourite with surfers and families alike.

It has a good beachside café and at Sennen Cove, the more popular southern end of the beach, is the Old Success Inn. Surfing equipment is available for hire and courses are also provided. ◈ *Map A5*

4 Kynance Cove
This is one of the best options on the Lizard Peninsula, where beaches are few and far between. The 10-minute walk from the car park is well worth the trudge for its fine white sands, rocky spires and surrounding grassy areas. Swimming is limited by the tides but other attractions include caves and cliffs with serpentine seams of sand. ◈ *Map B6*

5 Woolacombe Bay
Surf dudes come from far and wide to one of the West Country's most famous surfing beaches. The beach is popular with families and there is a warren of dunes behind for

The rocky shore at Kynance Cove

The beach at Fistral Bay

exploring. Crowds gather at the northern end, but more space can be found at the quieter southern end. The small resort of Woolacombe has shops and cafés (see p67).

Fistral Bay

Surf aficionados flock to this beach, which is the venue for surfing competitions. A surf centre supplies equipment for hire. Most of the sand is covered by water at high tide and strong currents mean that kids need to be careful, though lifeguards are present throughout the summer. The restaurants and cafés here offer outdoor seating. ◈ Map C4

Watergate Bay

North of Newquay, this arc of golden sand has a wild appeal. It is home to the Extreme Academy, which offers kite-surfing, land-boarding and other pursuits for the adventurous. Behind it are Jamie Oliver's famous restaurant, Fifteen, and the more casual Beach Hut (see p87), both with splendid views. Watergate is not very sheltered, so make sure you carry wind-breakers. ◈ Map C4

Tunnels Beach, Ilfracombe

This private beach is named after the tunnels that have provided access to it since 1823, when the swimming was segregated. There is a tidal bathing pool and on-duty lifeguards make the beach safe for kids. The rock pooling is top-class and there are kayaks for hire. ◈ Map H1 • Bath Place, Ilfracombe • 01271 879882 • Open Apr–Jun & Sep–Oct: 10am–6pm; Jul–Aug: 9am–9pm • Adm • www.tunnelsbeaches.co.uk

Croyde Bay

Sandwiched between the extensive west-facing Saunton Sands and Woolacombe, this compact bay has fine sand. There are campsites around and the village has pubs and bars that fill up in the evenings. ◈ Map H1

Blackpool Sands

Backed by woods and meadows, this family-friendly beach makes an enticing sight as it swings into view on the road from Dartmouth. Its sheltered location, clear water and fine sand makes this one of South Devon's best swimming spots. For refreshments there is the renowned Venus Café. ◈ Map K6

Left **Scones with jam and cream** Right **Rick Stein's Café, popular for fish and chips**

🔟 Culinary Specialities

1 Yarg Cheese
This moist cheese from Bodmin Moor has a covering of nettles and is the best known of a crop of Cornish cheeses to have appeared in recent years. There is also a version with a garlic flavour.

2 Star Gazy Pie
According to legend, this pie originated when Tom Bawcock, a fisherman from the Cornish village of Mousehole, braved fierce storms to provide fish for the starving villagers. Eaten on Tom Bawcock's Eve (December 23), the pie contains pilchards and five other kinds of fish, their heads poking through the crust, as if gazing skyward.

Devonshire pasties

3 Beer
Though Devon and Cornwall have traditionally been known for their cider consumption, local breweries have lately achieved fame for their real ale. St Austell is the biggest regional outfit, responsible for Tribute ale, which is exported nationwide. There are several excellent microbreweries as well, including Spingo made and drunk only in Helston (see p59).

4 Pilchards
Once the mainstay of the fishing industry in the West, pilchards had almost disappeared from local waters by 1914 due to being overfished. Since then, numbers have recovered but the catch is mostly exported. They can still be sampled in some restaurants, however, and are best eaten between July and November.

5 Cream Teas
The traditional cream tea consists of scones fresh from the oven, thickly churned clotted cream and lashings of strawberry jam. According to some, in

Charlotte's Victorian Tea House

Devon the cream is placed onto the half-scone first, then the jam; in Cornwall the jam is spread first and topped with cream.

Lobster
Lobster pots piled high in fishing ports attest to the abundance of lobster off the coasts of Devon and Cornwall. This delicacy can be barbecued or grilled, but usually tastes best simply boiled.

Pasties
Originally made for miners in Cornwall, this crimped pastry case with a meat and vegetable filling is ubiquitous in Devon too. The usual filling is beef, swede and potato, but can also be anything else. According to tradition, the top crimp is said to be Devonian in style, while the side crimp is authentically Cornish.

Wine
Sharpham in Devon and Camel Valley in Cornwall are two of Britain's most renowned wineries. Camel Valley also produces its own champagne-type fizz, "Cornwall".

Fish and Chips
The ports and resorts of Devon and Cornwall are among the best places to sample fish and chips. Superior outlets include Rick Stein's in Padstow (see pp30–31).

Crab
Some of the country's best crab comes from ports in Devon and Cornwall, such as Brixham and Port Isaac. Spider, blue velvet and brown crabs are the best varieties, and form the basis of a great salad or sandwich filling. Avoid eating them from January to March.

Top 10 Places for Cream Teas

1 Otterton Mill
Fine organic scones are made in this ancient mill. ⊗ Map L4 • Otterton, Budleigh Salterton • 01395 567041

2 Falmouth Hotel
Nibble scones on the terrace of this Victorian hotel. ⊗ Map C5 • Castle Beach, Falmouth • 01326 312671

3 New Yard, Trelowarren
Cream teas are served in this estate's stableyard. ⊗ Map B5 • Mawgan, Helston • 01326 221595

4 Charlotte's Victorian Tea House
Scrumptious teas in historic surroundings (see p95).

5 Primrose Cottage
Possibly Devon's best teas and cakes. ⊗ Map K5 • Lustleigh, Newton Abbot • 01647 277365

6 Southern Cross
A walled garden provides the perfect setting for tea. ⊗ Map L4 • Newton Poppleford, nr Sidmouth • 01395 568439

7 Georgian Tea Room
Choose from the selection of home-made cakes. ⊗ Map K4 • Broadway House, 35 High St, Topsham • 01392 873465

8 Stoke Barton Farm
This tea room offers fresh scones and cakes (see p71).

9 Trenance Cottage Tea Rooms
Nostalgia is the keynote here. ⊗ Map C4 • 2 Trenance Lane, Newquay • 01637 872034

10 Rectory Farm and Tea Rooms
Feast in a 13th-century farmhouse beside an open fire. ⊗ Map E2 • Crosstown, Morwenstow, near Bude • 01288 331251

For restaurants in the Devon and Cornwall region See pp71, 81, 87, 95 and 103.

Left **Tintagel Castle** Right **St Mawes Castle**

ⁱ⁰ Castles

1 Caerhays Castle
John Nash – architect of Buckingham Palace – designed this fantasy-Gothic structure in 1810, which is now a private home. The real showpiece is the garden, with its magnolias and rhododendrons. The adjacent curve of beach is also an excellent destination *(see p94)*.

2 Powderham Castle
This seat of the earls of Devon has been built in a mix of architectural styles. The dominant flavour is 18th-century, as seen in the ornate Music Room, designed by renowned architect James Wyatt, and the lavish Rococo Staircase Hall *(see p75)*.

3 Pendennis Castle
The most westerly of the artillery forts built under Henry VIII, Pendennis and its twin St Mawes were built to safeguard the port of Falmouth, the "key to Cornwall". The castle's ramparts and bastions were erected in around 1600 and the gun batteries were added during the Napoleonic wars *(see p97)*.

Powderham Castle

4 Berry Pomeroy Castle
This romantic ruin on the edge of a wooded ravine is reputed to be haunted. Built by the Pomeroy family in the 15th century, the castle was abandoned 200 years later. Ever since, there have been reported sightings of the ghosts of the "White Lady" and the "Blue Lady". ◈ *Map K5 • Totnes • 01803 866618 • Open late Mar–Jun & Sep: 10am–5pm daily; Jul & Aug: 10am–6pm daily; Oct: 10am–4pm daily • Adm • www.english-heritage.org.uk*

5 St Mawes Castle
The most elaborately decorated of Henry VIII's coastal fortresses, this castle follows a clover-leaf design, with round walls that were intended to deflect enemy fire. However, the castle was never tested in war – it surrendered without putting up a fight to Parliamentarian forces in 1646 *(see p34)*. Visitors can tour the gun rooms, governor's quarters, barracks and kitchen *(see p92)*.

Caerhays Castle

Castle Drogo

This 20th-century fortress in the Teign Valley was designed to resemble a medieval stronghold by architect Edwin Lutyens, who was instructed by retail tycoon Julius Drewe to create a replica of the castles of yore. Austere granite walls and a warren of stone corridors give the castle a spartan feel. You can play croquet here in summer *(see p12)*.

Okehampton Castle

The Norman castle on a spur above the River Okement is a dramatic sight, dominated by the remains of its keep. The fortress, once owned by the Courtenay family – later earls of Devon – was mainly used as a hunting lodge. Picnics can be enjoyed at the old deer park *(see p12)*.

Compton Castle

This buttressed manor house has been home to the seafaring Gilbert family – related to Sir Walter Raleigh – for nearly 600 years. Film-makers have long been attracted to its theatrical façade – Ang Lee filmed *Sense and Sensibility* here in 1995.
⬡ *Map K5 • Marldon, Paignton • 01803 843235 • Open Apr–Oct: 11am–5pm Mon, Wed & Thu • Adm • www.nationaltrust.org.uk*

Okehampton Castle

Tintagel Castle

Set on a promontory above the turbulent Atlantic, the forlorn ruins of Tintagel resemble a fairy-tale castle. Said to be the birthplace of the mythical King Arthur, the castle was in fact a Norman stronghold *(see p83)*.

Totnes Castle

Towering above the centre of Totnes, this classic Norman construction was erected after the Conquest *(see p34)* to overawe the Saxon town. The stone keep was added later. ⬡ *Map K5 • Totnes, Devon • 01803 864406 • Open late Mar–Jun & Sep: 10am–5pm daily; Jul & Aug: closes 6pm; Oct: closes 4pm • Adm • www.english-heritage.org.uk*

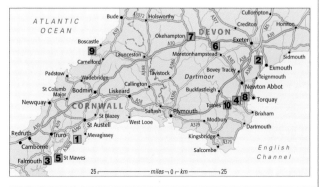

Left **Exeter Cathedral** Centre **Truro Cathedral** Right **St Neot's Church**

Churches, Abbeys and Cathedrals

St Nonna

Known as the "cathedral of the moors", this 15th-century church on Bodmin Moor is famous for its 79 bench-ends carved with saints, clowns and musicians. The Norman font with its fierce faces has been imitated in local churches. The "vicar of Altarnun" features in Daphne du Maurier's novel *Jamaica Inn*.
⊗ Map G4 • Altarnun
• 01566 86108

Truro Cathedral

Rising tall over Truro, this neo-Gothic monument was the first Anglican cathedral to be constructed in England since St Paul's in London. Built between 1880 and 1910, it incorporates the old parish church of St Mary's, which has occupied the spot for 600 years. Highlights include Jacobean tombs and Victorian stained glass *(see p92)*.

Exeter Cathedral

Surrounded by the grassy Cathedral Close and crowned by twin Norman towers, Exeter Cathedral is the grandest of Devon and Cornwall's churches. The 15th-century Exeter Clock and Chapter House, the 14th-century Minstrels' Gallery and carvings on the choir stalls are among the main attractions *(see pp20–21)*.

Buckfast Abbey

Buckfast Abbey

This complex on the banks of the River Dart was founded in the 11th century, rebuilt as a Cistercian abbey in 1147, dissolved in 1539 and rebuilt by Benedictine monks between 1907 and 1937. Today, visitors can admire the striking stained-glass windows of the new abbey and purchase home-made specialities made by the monks, such as tonic wine and beeswax *(see p80)*.

St Neot

Located in one of Bodmin Moor's prettiest villages, this 15th-century church contains stained-glass windows depicting Noah's Ark and St Neot himself. The churchyard boasts what is claimed to be Cornwall's finest ornamental cross. ⊗ Map E3 • St Neot, Cornwall • 01579 320472

St Nonna's Church

Church of the Holy Cross

The grandeur of this red sandstone structure reflects the former importance of Crediton, which grew wealthy on wool but is now just a village. The church is perpendicular in style, with generous windows illuminating its rich interior. The Chapter House displays 17th-century armour and weaponry *(see p76)*.

St Mary

Set on a hill in poet Samuel Taylor Coleridge's native town, stately St Mary dates from the 13th century. It was enlarged a century later by John de Grandisson, Bishop of Exeter. Noteworthy features include a still working 14th-century astronomical clock and the Apostles Window, the church's exquisite west window. ✪ *Map L3 • College Rd, Ottery St Mary • 01404 812062 • www.otterystmary.org.uk*

St Just-in-Roseland

Situated on the Roseland peninsula, this church on the shore of a creek is surrounded by palms and magnolias. The church dates from 1261, but its battlement tower was added in the 15th-century. ✪ *Map C5 • St Just-in-Roseland • 01326 270248 • www.stjustinroseland.org.uk*

The façade of St Mary

St Enodoc

This tiny 13th-century church is located in the middle of a golf course within sight of the Camel Estuary. The churchyard holds the grave of the poet John Betjeman who lived for a time in nearby Trebetherick *(see p86)*.

St Petroc

Built around 1470, the largest parish church in Cornwall has a typical Cornish wagon roof. Look out for the Vyvian tomb, an effigy carved from Catacleuse stone in the 1530s. The Norman font shows angels, demons and interlacing trees of life *(see p30)*.

Left **Boathouse at Trevarno** Right **Bicton Park**

⓾ Great Gardens

1 Lost Gardens of Heligan
There is an air of mystery about this "lost garden". First planted in the late-18th century, the garden was neglected to the point of decay until it was rediscovered by Tim Smit, the guiding light behind the Eden Project *(see pp10–11)*. Smit restored the garden's main features while preserving its wild, tangled character. The site includes an Italian Garden, walled flower gardens and a subtropical "Jungle" valley *(see p91)*.

2 Trelissick Garden
Sheltered by woodlands, this Cornish garden features the national collection of photinias and azaras. Bordering the River Fal, the site affords views across the Carrick Roads Estuary *(see p93)*.

3 Trevarno
Visitors to this garden can enjoy a wealth of attractions including the sunken Italian

The jungle in the Lost Gardens of Heligan

Garden, a century-old Yew Tunnel, carpets of bluebells, a rockery and a grotto. But for horticulturalists, the highlight is the National Museum of Gardening, which has the country's largest collection of gardening antiques. ⓢ *Map B5*
• *Sithney, Helston* • *01326 574274*
• *Open 10:30am–5pm daily* • *Adm*
• *www.trevarno.co.uk*

4 Trebah
The subtropical garden has water gardens with Koi carp and glades of 100-year-old tree ferns. Plants have been introduced from around the world, including Gunnera (giant rhubarb) from Brazil and New Zealand flax. Rhododendrons and hydrangeas lead to a private beach on the River Helford. ⓢ *Map C5* • *Mawnan Smith* • *01326 252200* • *Open 10:30am–6:30pm daily* • *Adm; half price for bus arrivals* • *www.trebahgarden.co.uk*

5 Tresco Abbey Gardens
First planted in 1834, these gardens, located in the Isles of Scilly, have been carefully nurtured by five generations of the same family. The region's climate, the mildest in the UK, has made it possible to cultivate exotic plants from around the southern hemisphere. The Tresco Abbey ruins are an evocative backdrop to the lush gardens *(see pp22–3)*.

A stunning flower border at Rosemoor

Mount Edgcumbe

8 On the Rame Peninsula outside Plymouth, Mount Edgcumbe has Italian, French and American formal gardens and is home to the national camellia collection, which flowers from January. The parklands include follies and a deer park *(see p14)*.

Glendurgan

6 This wooded valley garden on the banks of the Helford has walled areas and herbaceous growths with brilliant colour and foliage. The spring-flowering magnolias and camellias are especially impressive. Children will enjoy the baffling laurel maze dating from 1833 and the Giant's Stride rope swing. Ⓢ *Map C5*
• *Mawnan Smith* • *01326 250906* • *Open mid-Feb–Jul & Sep–Oct: 10:30am–5:30pm Tue–Sat & hols; Aug: also open Mon* • *Adm* • *www.nationaltrust.org.uk*

Rosemoor

7 In North Devon's Torridge Valley, RHS Rosemoor holds year-round interest, with snow-drops in winter, rhododendrons in spring, flower borders in summer and fiery hues in autumn. The most spectacular displays, however, are 2,000 roses with over 200 cultivars. Model gardens and woodland walks provide further interest. Ⓢ *Map H2*
• *Great Torrington* • *01805 624067* • *Open Apr–Sep: 10am–6pm daily; Oct–Mar: 10am–5pm daily* • *Adm, RHS members free* • *www.rhs.org.uk*

Lanhydrock

9 Surrounding this grand manor house are horticultural spectacles, including a unique yew-hedged herbaceous garden, at its best in summer. Other highlights are magnolias from Sikkim, Tibet and southern China, hybrid rhododendrons and geraniums *(see pp8–9)*.

Bicton Park

10 This extensive estate has formal parterres of bedding plants and a renowned collection of trees, including a giant Grecian Fir. The elegant Palm House, dating from the 1820s, holds rare palms, while the Tropical House features the Bicton orchid. A woodland railway provides scenic rides through the landscaped park *(see p78)*.

The Royal Horticultural Society (RHS) is the world's leading horticultural body and the UK's biggest gardening charity.

49

Left **Prideaux Place** Right **Pencarrow House**

🔟 Great Houses

1 Trerice
An architectural gem with ornate fireplaces and elaborate ceilings, this small Elizabethan manor has a good collection of English furniture, clocks and examples of needlework. The highlight is the barrel ceiling of its Great Chamber. The hayloft outside holds a quirky lawn-mower museum *(see p86).*

2 Pencarrow
This 18th-century mansion is noted for its porcelain and paintings, including portraits by Joshua Reynolds *(see p57)*. The bedrooms upstairs display costumes used by actors in films shot here. Alfresco performances are staged in the grounds in summer *(see p83).*

3 Cotehele House
Hidden in the byways of the Tamar Valley, this Tudor palace is a must for all fans of embroidery, with the bedrooms adorned in heavy tapestries – the absence of electric lights has helped to preserve these. The house also has four-poster beds and finely crafted furniture. It is best to visit on a sunny day *(see p93).*

4 Prideaux Place
The Prideaux family has occupied this fine manor house since 1592. It holds many treasures, including loot from the Spanish Armada and the country's oldest cast-iron cannon. The grounds include a deer park, a grotto and a 9th-century Celtic cross *(see p30).*

5 Hartland Abbey
The abbey, founded in 1157, was the last one in England to fall victim to the Dissolution of the Monasteries *(see p34)*, and has since been a private home. Today, its architecture and decoration range from medieval to Victorian-Gothic. Highlights include the vaulted Alhambra

Lanhydrock Garden

Corridor and the Regency library, which has portraits by Gainsborough and Reynolds.
📍 *Map G2 • Hartland, Bideford • 01237 441264 • Open Apr–late-May: 2–5pm Wed, Thu, Sun & hols; late-May–early-Oct: 2–5pm Sun–Thu; grounds open at noon • Adm • www.hartlandabbey.com*

Buckland Abbey
Founded as a Cistercian abbey in 1278, Buckland Abbey was dissolved by Henry VIII, converted into a private home by the distinguished mariner Richard Grenville and acquired by Francis Drake in 1580. Drake's seafaring exploits are related here and visitors can admire the Great Barn, which is bigger than the house itself *(see p77)*.

Saltram
The grandiose exterior of this 18th-century mansion set in parkland outside Plymouth is matched by the succession of stately rooms inside, each decorated with a dazzling array of art. The most opulent is the Great Drawing Room, designed by Robert Adam *(see p14)*.

St Michael's Mount
This rocky island was linked with Normandy's Mont St Michel until 1424 and later became a fortified private home. The best-preserved parts are the Chevy Chase Room, the 14th-century church and the Lady Chapel, later converted into a drawing room *(see p28)*.

Knightshayes Court
The original designer of this Victorian country pile was flamboyant architect

The dining room at Hartland Abbey

William Burges. When costs began to rocket, Burges was sacked, but enough of his Gothic-style interiors remain including in the library, vaulted hall and the arched red drawing room. 📍 *Map K2 • Bolham, Tiverton • 01884 254665 • Open mid-Feb–late Feb: 11am–4pm Sat–Thu; mid-Mar–early Nov: closes 5pm; garden: open daily • Adm • www.nationaltrust.org.uk*

Lanhydrock
This 17th-century palace was rebuilt in the high Victorian style after a fire in 1881, but the North Wing containing the Jacobean Long Gallery and the gatehouse survived. The building is filled with accoutrements of a 19th-century mansion, including the elaborate kitchens *(see pp8–9)*.

Left **National Seal Sanctuary** Centre **The Land's End Experience** Right **A tamarin, Newquay Zoo**

🔟 Children's Attractions

1 National Seal Sanctuary
In this rescue centre, watch recovered and orphaned seals frolic in outdoor pools. Children will be especially charmed by the seal pups. Dolphins and turtles are occasionally brought here, and the centre also cares for donkeys, ponies and goats. Feeding times and talks are popular daily events *(see p100)*.

2 Flambards
The attractions at this complex include a recreated Victorian Village and Britain in the Blitz. Thrills are provided by the Hornet Roller Coaster and the Canyon River Log Flume, while the Science Park offers interactive fun. Fireworks are set off on Wednesday evenings in August.
🅂 *Map B5* • *Helston, Cornwall*
• *08456 018684* • *Open mid-Mar–late Jul: 10:30am–5pm daily; late Jul–Aug 10am–5:30pm daily; Sep–late Oct: 10:30am–4:30pm daily* • *Adm*
• *www.flambards.co.uk*

3 Babbacombe Model Village
Children will love this miniature, all-weather world which includes railways, an animated circus and a model castle with a fire-breathing dragon. After dusk, 10,000 bulbs light up the streets, homes and gardens. 🅂 *Map K5*
• *Hampton Ave, Babbacombe, Torquay*
• *01803 315315* • *Opening times vary, check website for details* • *Adm*
• *www.babbacombemodelvillage.co.uk*

4 The Monkey Sanctuary
This charitable sanctuary overlooking Looe Bay promotes the welfare of South American woolly and capuchin monkeys. A colony of lesser horseshoe bats housed here can be observed via cameras and infra-red lights. The eco-friendly Tree Top Café offers delicious vegetarian food. 🅂 *Map G5*
• *St Martin's, Looe* • *01503 262532*
• *Open mid-Mar–Sep: 11am–4:30pm Sun–Thu* • *Adm* • *www.monkeysanctuary.org*

Miniature houses, Babbacombe Model Village

Newquay Zoo

Cornwall's only zoo is set in lakeside gardens and houses lions, pumas, meerkats and armadillos. Activities for kids include the Tarzan Trail and the Dragon Maze. Special events take place through the year *(see p83)*.

Paignton Zoo

Gorillas and gibbons are among the highlights at this zoo. Many animals can be viewed from the Jungle Express miniature railway. Recreated environments include the Crocodile Swamp, which is home to crocodiles from Cuba *(see p78)*.

Land's End Experience

Located at mainland Britain's most westerly point, this theme park offers audiovisual exhibitions, including *Return to the Last Labyrinth*, which explores legends associated with the headland. Kids can get close to animals at Greeb Farm. ◈ Map A5 • Sennen • 08717 200055 • Open late May–mid-Sep: 10am–4pm; mid-Sep–late May: call to check opening times • Adm • www.landsend-landmark.co.uk

Watermouth Castle

This Victorian folly castle and adventure park includes a model railway, water gardens and a Snake Tube Slide. The castle itself displays suits of armour. Beware of the expensive slot machines in the dungeons. ◈ Map H1 • Berrynarbor, Ilfracombe • 01271 867474 • Open late Mar–late May, Jun–late Jul & Sep–Oct: 10:30am–5:30pm Sun–Fri; late May & late Jul–Aug: 10am–6:30pm Sun–Fri • Adm • www. watermouthcastle.com

An exhibition at Future World @ Goonhilly

Future World @ Goonhilly

This satellite station at Goonhilly Downs on the Lizard Peninsula tells the story of international communications through film shows, artifacts and interactive displays. You can "email an alien" in the Multimedia Visitor Centre, operate a satellite dish and enjoy snacks at the Big Dish Café *(see p100)*.

Living Coasts

Focusing on the conservation of coastal and marine life, this aquatic zoo features the flora and fauna that are found along Britain's coasts. Visitors can learn about a range of birds and mammals and the ecological issues affecting them. Living exhibits include avocets, puffins and cormorants, though the penguin beach and seal amphitheatre are perennial favourites *(see p75)*.

Left **Museum of North Devon** Right **The Wayside Museum**

🔟 Museums

1 Overbeck's Museum
Scientist Otto Overbeck lived here until 1937. Many of his eccentric inventions, such as a "rejuvenating machine", share space with exhibits on local history. The garden has exotic plants and offers superb coastal views *(see p78)*.

2 Royal Cornwall Museum
Cornwall's county museum addresses local geology and culture, with collections of insects on display alongside Roman coins found in the area. Buddhist figures from Burma and an unwrapped Egyptian mummy are also on display *(see p91)*.

Honiton lace on show at Allhallows Museum

3 Museum of Dartmoor Life
Housed in a former granary, this museum illustrates aspects of the moor and its inhabitants, from prehistoric hut-dwellers to the tin-mining communities *(see p12)*.

Trewinnard coach, Royal Cornwall Museum

4 Allhallows Museum
Honiton was famous for lace-making between the 16th and 18th centuries. As well as displays of lovely specimens of lace, this museum also showcases fossilized bones of the Honiton hippos, mementos of clock- and cream-making and local pottery *(see p78)*.

5 The Wayside Museum
This eclectic jumble of memorabilia is like a bulging scrapbook of West Cornwall life. Exhibits include pestles and mortars from 3,000 BC, a reconstructed Victorian parlour and displays illustrating occupations such as fishing, mining and smuggling. Copious cuttings and photographs provide a fascinating background *(see p100)*.

6 National Marine Aquarium
Part traditional aquarium and part 21st-century museum, this complex offers an awe-inspiring survey of ocean life. Over 50 live exhibits contain some 4,000 examples of marine life *(see p14)*.

7 Museum of North Devon
This museum is the perfect place to gain an insight into North Devon's history. Exhibits include locally minted Saxon

Display at the National Maritime Museum

coins, a 17th-century kiln and local pottery. The region's natural history is well represented and part of the museum is devoted to local militaria (see p69).

National Maritime Museum, Cornwall
This museum displays boats from around the world, nautical equipment, interactive displays and marine art. The centrepiece is the grand Flotilla Gallery, where small craft hang from the roof (see p100).

Fairlynch Museum
Fossils, prehistoric flints, 18th-century costumes, and collections of lace and toys at this museum help to create a picture of life in South Devon through the ages. The building is a fascinating exhibit in itself – a thatched *cottage orné* built by a local shipowner (see p78).

Helston Folk Museum
This museum focuses on the social history of Helston and the Lizard Peninsula. It has sections dedicated to telegraphy pioneer Marconi and the locally born boxing champion Bob Fitzsimmons (1863–1917). ⊗ Map B5 • Market Place, Helston • 01326 564027 • Open 10am–1pm Mon–Sat, to 4pm in school hols • Adm, free Sat

Top 10 Art Galleries

Tate St Ives
Absorb past and present artistic trends at this seaside gallery (see p26).

The Exchange
The latest addition to the Penzance art scene (see p28).

Newlyn Art Gallery
View modern works of art at this old fishing port. ⊗ Map A5 • New Road, Newlyn • 01736 363715 • www.newlynartgallery.co.uk

Burton Art Gallery and Museum
Paintings and prized local slipware are exhibited here. (see p67).

Barbara Hepworth Museum and Sculpture Garden
View sculptures in Hepworth's beautiful garden (see p26).

St Ives Society of Artists Gallery
This private gallery shows rotating exhibitions of local artists (see p26).

Broomhill Sculpture Gardens
Part hotel and restaurant, part gallery and sculpture garden showing contemporary works. ⊗ Map H2 • Muddiford Rd, Barnstaple • 01271 850262 • Adm • www.broomhillart.co.uk

Falmouth Art Gallery
A strong collection of works by artists with local links. ⊗ Map C5 • The Moor, Falmouth • 01326 313863 • www.falmouthartgallery.com

Penlee House
The best place to see paintings of the Newlyn School (see p28).

Torre Abbey Mansion
A broad selection of high-quality art in Torquay's oldest building (see p76).

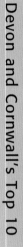

Left **Sir Arthur Conan Doyle** Right **Agatha Christie**

🔟 Famous Writers

1 D. H. Lawrence

D. H. Lawrence spent the years 1915–17 in the remote village of Zennor with his wife Frieda. He loved the "high shaggy moor hills, and big sweep of lovely sea", but was forced to leave in the face of hostility. He later described his Cornish experiences in the novel *Kangaroo*.

2 Sir Arthur Conan Doyle

Dartmoor provided the inspiration for Conan Doyle's yarn, *The Hound of the Baskervilles*, based on a number of local legends concerning supernatural black dogs that inhabited the remotest reaches of the moor.

3 Charles Causley

Along with John Betjeman, Causley is one of the best known 20th-century poets associated with Cornwall. He was born and brought up in Launceston, returning to live there in 1946. His work drew on hymns and ballads, and described Cornish life and legends.

4 R D Blackmore

Although he wrote a number of novels, Blackmore is remembered today only for his swash-buckling romance, *Lorna Doone* (1869), set on Exmoor in the 17th century. Fans can visit scenes described in this tale of the evil Doone clan, including the Valley of the Rocks outside Lynmouth.

R D Blackmore

5 Agatha Christie

Born in Torquay, the "Mistress of Murder" spent much of her life in South Devon, particularly in Greenway, a grand mansion overlooking the River Dart. The settings of her country-house whodunits have a strong flavour of the area. Torquay Museum has a good exhibition devoted to her.

Max Gate in Dorset, Thomas Hardy's home

6 Thomas Hardy

For Hardy, Cornwall was "the region of dream and mystery". Although he is more associated with Dorset, it was at Boscastle on the North Cornwall coast that he worked as an architect and met his first wife, Emma. His novel, *A Pair of Blue Eyes*, is set there.

Daphne du Maurier

Top 10 Artists in Devon and Cornwall

1 Joshua Reynolds
Born and raised near Plymouth, Reynolds was one of the foremost portrait artists of the 18th century.

2 Elizabeth Forbes
Born in Canada in 1859, the Newlyn painter is best known for her portrayal of children.

3 Stanhope Forbes
Husband of Elizabeth Forbes, the Irish-born artist was a leading figure of the Newlyn school.

4 Norman Garstin
His most famous work, *The Rain It Raineth Everyday* (1889), is on display in Penlee House, Penzance.

5 Alfred Wallis
A simple fisherman "discovered" by the St Ives artists, Wallis is known for his naïve style.

6 Bernard Leach
A higly influential potter, Leach was based for a long time in St Ives.

7 Barbara Hepworth
The St Ives studio of this sculptor is now a gallery displaying her works.

8 Ben Nicholson
Barbara Hepworth's husband exerted great influence with his austere, abstract paintings.

9 Terry Frost
One of Britain's most prominent abstract painters, Terry Frost was based mainly in St Ives and Newlyn.

10 Patrick Heron
His highly coloured abstract works are typified by his giant stained-glass window in the Tate St Ives.

7 Sir Arthur Quiller-Couch
"Q" was a famed literary critic, poet and author. He set many of his tales in Fowey, which appeared as "Troy" in his books. Visitors to Fowey can see a memorial to Q on the Hall Walk (see p36). He was Professor of English at Cambridge University.

8 Henry Williamson
The novelist and naturalist set his classic animal tale, *Tarka the Otter*, in the lush countryside of North Devon. The book has been the inspiration of the Tarka Trail, a recreational route around the Taw and Torridge rivers.

9 Winston Graham
All 12 of Graham's Poldark novels, written between 1945 and 2002, were set mainly around Perranporth, but also took in other parts of Cornwall including Mousehole and Lanhydrock. The books enjoyed great success as TV adaptations in the 1970s.

10 Daphne du Maurier
Having spent many childhood holidays in Cornwall, du Maurier eventually settled outside Fowey. Drawn to Cornwall's secluded creeks and the wild romance of the moors, she set some of her famous novels here – including *Rebecca* and *Jamaica Inn*. An annual literary festival celebrates her work (see p38).

Left **Ship Inn**, Exeter Right **Exterior of the Mason's Arms**

Pubs

Ship Inn, Exeter
Steps away from Exeter Cathedral, this inn was once Sir Francis Drake's *(see p17)* local haunt. The nautical theme is strong with maps, knots and clay pipes. Simple meals are served in the low-ceilinged bar or the restaurant upstairs. ⊛ *Map P2 • 1–3 Martins Lane, Exeter • 01392 272040*

Tinners Arms
This historic pub dates from 1271 and is a fine place for a drink and a meal. There is a warming log fire in winter and it hosts live music on most Thursdays. Children are also welcome. D. H. Lawrence *(see p56)* stayed here when he came to live in Zennor *(see p102)*.

Blisland Inn
A traditional country pub on Bodmin Moor, Blisland Inn has Toby jugs hanging from wooden beams and walls festooned with photographs. A good choice of real ales and tasty food makes this a very popular spot *(see p87)*.

Ship Inn, Mousehole
This excellent inn stands right above the harbour in a tiny fishing village. The Tinners and Tribute ales and the seafood platter

are worth sampling. If you miss out on a seat with harbour views, sit in the tiny patio garden upstairs. Accommodation is available *(see p102)*.

Warren House Inn
The third-highest pub in England stands in solitary splendour on Dartmoor. It is a welcome sight to walkers, with two hearths – one that has reputedly been kept burning since 1845 – and good, inexpensive food. ⊛ *Map J4 • 4 km (2 miles) NE of Postbridge, Dartmoor • 01822 880208*

A toby jug at the Blisland Inn

Blue Anchor Inn
One of the best pubs in the West, Blue Anchor Inn is worth going out of your way for its Spingo bitters. The building is a former monks' resthouse divided into many small rooms. The pub has friendly staff and manages a B&B next door *(see p102)*.

Ship Inn, Mousehole

The interior of the Admiral Benbow

Admiral Benbow
Steeped in history, this pub is decorated with anchors and ships' figureheads. The well-kept beer and good food ensures a steady clientele – so get here early if you don't want to wait to eat. Look out for the straw smuggler on the roof *(see p102)*.

Turk's Head
Said to be Penzance's oldest pub, Turk's Head dates from 1233 and has as a maze of low-ceilinged rooms, a beer garden and a smugglers' tunnel leading to the harbour. Real ales include Wadworth's and Sharp's. ◈ *Map B5 • Chapel St, Penzance • 01736 363093*

Mason's Arms
Located 10 minutes from the beach, this East Devon inn dispenses great locally brewed bitters and serves top-notch food, including local lobster and crab. You can sit outside under thatched table umbrellas too. Rooms are available. ◈ *Map M4 • Branscombe, Devon • 01297 680300*

Bridge Inn
The pink-walled, 16th-century Bridge Inn with real ales and traditional trappings is one of Devon's best. It is reputedly the only pub to have been graced by the Queen in an official capacity, when she visited in 1998. ◈ *Map K4 • Bridge Hill, Topsham • 01392 873862*

Top 10 Local Ales

Skinners
This Truro-based brewery features ales named after Cornish folk heroes, such as Betty Stogs.

St Austell
This is Cornwall's major brewer, whose traditional cask ales include the legendary HSD and Tribute.

Sharp's
The Cornish producer of such fine beers as Doom Bar, Cornish Coaster and Eden.

Otter
A Honiton-based brewery, which produces four regular beers and one winter ale available throughout Devon.

O'Hanlon's
In Devon since 2000, this small, specialist brewery produces award-winning cask and bottled beers.

Country Life
Bideford-based producer of ales such as Old Appledore, the light-coloured Pot Wallop and the heady Country Bumpkin.

Spingo Ales
This famous brew is available only in Helston's Blue Anchor, in four distinctive varieties from 4.5 per cent to 6.5 per cent ABV.

Coastal Brewery
Beers of this Redruth brewery can be found in select pubs in the region.

Ales of Scilly
Scilly-based producer of Firebrand and Scuppered bitters, in addition to some seasonal beers.

Organic Brewhouse
This was the first brewery in Britain to produce solely organic real ales. It operates from the Lizard Peninsula.

For more pubs **See p103.**

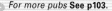

Left **Tavistock Pannier Market** Right **Cornwall Crafts Association**

Shopping

Totnes Elizabethan Market
Every Tuesday morning throughout summer, local traders don Tudor costumes for the Elizabethan market, which runs alongside an all-day craft market. ◈ *Map K5 • Civic Square, Totnes • 01803 863168 • Open May–Sep*

Barnstaple Pannier Market
A lively market is held daily until around 4pm in this purpose-built hall dating from 1855. Come for books, clothing, household goods, local produce, crafts and antiques *(see p69)*.

Devon Guild of Craftsmen
This consortium sells some of the best contemporary crafts made in the region, including ceramics, basketwork, jewellery and furniture. Its base at the edge of Dartmoor holds regular exhibitions. ◈ *Map K4 • Riverside Mill, Bovey Tracey • 01626 832223*

Devon Guild of Craftsmen

Kingsbridge Markets
The Kingsbridge town hall hosts a flea market on Mondays (May–Oct), a country produce market on Wednesday mornings, a CD fair on Saturdays (Apr–Sep) and a craft market on Fridays (Apr–Dec). Down at the quay, a farmers' market is held on the first and third Saturday of the month. ◈ *Map J6 • Fore St, Kingsbridge*

Dartington Cider Press Centre
Cider-making stopped 50 years ago, but local cider can still be purchased at this complex of shops in the grounds of Dartington Hall. The site also holds a Cranks vegetarian restaurant. A local produce market is held every Saturday. ◈ *Map J5 • Shinners Bridge, Dartington • 01803 847500 • www. dartington.org/cider-press-centre*

Tavistock Pannier Market
Tavistock's indoor market is open on most days of the week. It offers antiques and collectables (Tuesdays), crafts (Wednesdays and Thursdays), local produce (Fridays), mixed markets (first and third Saturday of the month) and a Victorian market (fourth Saturday). ◈ *Map H4 • Tavistock • 01822 611003*

Dartington Cider Press Centre

Duchy of Cornwall Nursery

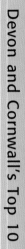

Duchy of Cornwall Nursery

One of the largest nurseries in the Southwest, this place is an inspiration to gardeners, offering a range of shrubs, ornamental and fruit trees, climbers and conservatory plants. Specialities include conifers, fuchsias, bamboos and camellias. ◎ *Map E4*
• *Cott Road, Lostwithiel • 01208 872668*
• *www.duchyofcornwallnursery.co.uk*

Cornwall Crafts Association

A range of top quality Cornish arts and crafts are exhibited and sold at two locations. The goods give an idea about contemporary trends. ◎ *Trelowarren: Map B5*
• *Mawgan-in-Meneage, Helston • 01326 221567; Trelissick Gardens: Map C5*
• *Trelissick, Feock, Truro • 01872 864514*
• *www.cornwallcrafts.co.uk*

Bickleigh Mill

A working 18-century watermill is the venue for this retail centre, which sells eco-friendly clothing, silverware, Dartington glass and original art. ◎ *Map K3 • Bickleigh, Tiverton • 01884 855419 • www.bickleighmill.com*

St Ives Art Galleries

St Ives is a magnet for art enthusiasts, not just for established names exhibited in the Tate and the myriad smaller galleries. Styles and quality vary, as do the prices *(see p26)*.

Top 10 Things to Buy

1 Local Art
Buy local art at small galleries, which are to Devon and Cornwall what antique shops are to the Cotswolds.

2 Serpentine
A speciality of the Lizard Peninsula, this greenish rock is used to make a variety of local ornaments.

3 Fudge
Creamy and delicious flavoured fudge is available in almost all gift shops throughout the region.

4 Ice cream
Most resorts have at least one shop selling quality ice cream in a range of contemporary flavours.

5 Local Wine and Gin
West Country wines are among the country's finest, while Plymouth gin is internationally famous.

6 Fishermen's Apparel
Fishing smocks, caps and woolly jumpers make great mementos and souvenirs.

7 Crafts
Hand-crafted woodwork, jewellery, silverware and glassware are among the West's specialities.

8 Fresh Seafood
Experience the thrill of buying seafood directly from the harbour. It can usually be iced and packaged for the ride back home.

9 Surf Gear
All the major surf gear brands are represented at outlets in the surfing centres of Devon and Cornwall.

10 Pottery
Some of the country's most renowned potters are based in the West and exhibit their wares.

Left **A train on the Liskeard-to-Looe line** Right **The Paignton-Kingswear Railway line**

🔟 Great Train Rides

1 Exeter to Newton Abbot

From Exeter, the main line runs beside two estuaries, the Exe and the Teign, offering delightful vistas over the serene mudflats populated by wading birds.
🚶 *Map K4* • *08457 484950*

2 Tarka Line

Named after *Tarka the Otter* which was largely set around here, this 65-km (39-mile) line weaves through Devon's rural heartland. After Crediton, it sticks close to the River Taw, passing through woodlands inhabited by great spotted and green woodpeckers, and buzzards. 🚶 *Map H1* • *08457 484950*

3 The Dartmoor Line

The line running between Exeter and Okehampton provides a handy way to reach Dartmoor quickly, taking around 45 minutes. Only two bicycles can be carried on each train. 🚶 *Map K3*
• *08457 484950* • *Open May–Sep: Sun*

4 Bodmin and Wenford Railway

The steam or diesel engines of this private standard-gauge line provide an excellent way to explore the country around Bodmin. The terminus at Bodmin Parkway is linked by a 3-km (2-mile) path to Lanhydrock *(see pp8–9)*. There is direct access to the Camel Trail from Boscarne Junction and to Cardinham Woods from Colesloggett Halt. 🚶 *Map J4*
• *08451 259678* • *www. bodminandwenfordrailway.co.uk*

5 Looe Valley Line

The fishing port of Looe is linked to Liskeard by this branch line dating from 1860. The route passes through the heavily wooded Looe Valley. 🚶 *Map G5*
• *08457 484950*

6 Tamar Valley Line

This branch line meanders through the Tamar Valley. The highlight is the Calstock Viaduct

The Bodmin and Wenford Steam Railway

Check www.nationalrail.co.uk for train information, unless otherwise shown.

crossing between Devon and Cornwall. A "rail ale trail" is available for visiting pubs along the way. ◈ *Map F2* • *08457 484950*

7 South Devon Railway
From a station outside Totnes, steam trains of the South Devon Railway depart several times daily, between April and October (and some dates in winter), for a scenic ride to Buckfastleigh, on the edge of Dartmoor. There is a stop at Staverton, with access to a path beside the River Dart *(see p80)*.

8 Launceston Steam Railway
These narrow-gauged steam engines from Victoria's reign run for 4 km (3 miles) between Launceston and Newmills. At Launceston Station you can wander around the railway workshops, an engineering museum and an Augustinian Priory.
◈ *Map G4* • *01566 775665*
• *www.launcestonsr.co.uk*

9 Paignton and Dartmouth Steam Railway
This heritage line runs along the Tor Bay coast from Paignton Station before chugging alongside the River Dart to Kingswear. A "round robin" ticket includes a river cruise from Dartmouth to Totnes as well as a coach back to the town of Paignton.
◈ *Map K5* • *01803 555872*
• *www.paignton-steamrailway.co.uk*

10 St Erth to St Ives
This picturesque branch line is the best way to reach St Ives *(see pp26–7)*. It edges along the Hayle Estuary before winding around the beaches of St Ives Bay, ending up steps away from Porthminster Beach. ◈ *Map B5*
• *08457 484950*

Top 10 Beauty Spots

1 Lydford Gorge, Dartmoor
This lovely spot offers riverside walks, a whirlpool and a waterfall *(see p12)*.

2 Hartland Point
Cliffs and crags flank this promontory with views of Lundy Island *(see p70)*.

3 Roseland Peninsula
One of the region's most photogenic, least spoilt spots, with two waterside churches *(see p91)*.

4 Valley of the Rocks, Exmoor
This dry valley has striking rock formations and coastal views *(see p70)*.

5 Golitha Falls, Bodmin Moor
A series of waterfall cascades gush through oak and beech woodland. ◈ *Map G4*

6 Lizard Point
A wild, rocky promontory at England's southern tip, with invigorating walks to beaches. ◈ *Map C6*

7 Watersmeet, Exmoor
A canopy of oaks covers this confluence of the East Lyn and Hoar Oak rivers. Ideal for walks *(see p70)*.

8 Cape Cornwall, Penwith Peninsula
The ocean pounds against this craggy headland, overlooked by an abandoned chimney stack. ◈ *Map A5*

9 Dartmeet, Dartmoor
The West and East Dart rivers merge here, right by a "clapper" bridge and close to a nature reserve *(see p13)*.

10 Hell Bay, Isles of Scilly
On the island of Bryher, this dramatic and stunning bay bears the full brunt of Atlantic storms. ◈ *Map A4*

AROUND TOWN

DEVON AND CORNWALL'S TOP 10

Left **Museum of North Devon** Right **Boat moored on the beach at Appledore**

North Devon

BETWEEN THE AUSTERE HEIGHTS OF EXMOOR *and the rocky pinnacles of Hartland Point, North Devon crams in a rich landscape. Two of the region's top nature reserves, Northam Burrows and Braunton Burrows, and some of the best beaches, such as Woolacombe Bay, Saunton Sands and Westward Ho! are located on this stretch of coast. The main towns are Barnstaple, Ilfracombe and Bideford, but the true treasures are the coastal villages of Appledore and Clovelly. Inland, the Tarka Trail is ideal for cycling or walking, while out at sea, Lundy Island is home to puffins and seals.*

Scenic Croyde Bay near the town of Barnstaple

10 Sights

1. Tarka Trail
2. Woolacombe Bay
3. Braunton Burrows
4. Burton Art Gallery and Museum
5. Appledore
6. Clovelly
7. Museum of North Devon
8. Lynton and Lynmouth
9. Barnstaple Pannier Market
10. Lundy Island

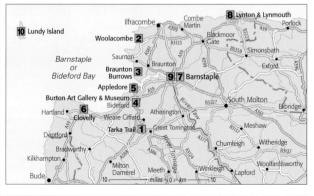

Preceding pages **The magnificent nave in Exeter Cathedral**

Surfers at Woolacombe Bay

Tarka Trail

Henry Williamson's classic animal fable, *Tarka the Otter (see p68)*, was set around his native North Devon. The otter's epic journeys are traced in this 300-km (180-miles) trail, which describes a figure of eight centring on the town of Barnstaple and incorporating sections of the South West Coast Path and the Tarka Line railway. Over 50 km (30 miles) of the trail, between Braunton and Meeth, can be cycled. Other sections take in the scenic Taw Valley and Williamson's home village of Georgeham.
⊗ Map H1–H3

Woolacombe Bay

Surfers know this impressive arc of sand as one of the country's top sites for riding the waves, but non-surfers will find plenty of elbow room here, especially at the more sheltered southern end, Putsborough. Surf equipment can be rented at shops and stalls above the beach, where there are also a handful of cafés and bars.
⊗ Map H1

Braunton Burrows

The core of a UN-designated biosphere, this wild and wind-blown area constitutes the largest sand-dune system in the UK. The dunes are stabilized by marram grass and a range of other plants. More than 400 recorded species of vascular plants and a great variety of invertebrate species make their home here. The area is traversed by meandering paths, and can be reached on the Tarka Trail and the South West Coast Path *(see pp36–7)*. ⊗ Map H2

Burton Art Gallery and Museum

The "little white town" of Bideford, rich with historical associations and home of the Elizabethan mariner Sir Richard Grenville, houses the Burton Art Gallery and Museum. The gallery boasts an absorbing collection of art and artifacts including Colin Hunter's atmospheric painting, *Kelp Gatherers*, and examples of the famed local slipware. The museum is located in Victoria Park, which holds cannons taken from the Spanish Armada *(see p17)*. ⊗ Map H2 • Kingsley Road, Bideford • 01237 471455 • Open 10am–5pm Mon–Fri, 10am–4pm Sat, 11am–4pm Sun • www.burtonartgallery.co.uk

Pottery at Burton Art Gallery and Museum

The settlement of Clovelly tumbling down to a small harbour

steep main street unmanageable. Some of the cottages are open to the public, including a museum dedicated to Charles Kingsley, author of *The Water Babies*, who lived here as a child. ⊗ *Map G2 • Tourist information: 01237 431781 • www.clovelly.co.uk*

Appledore

A stately air hangs over this off-the-beaten-track settlement of Georgian houses at the edge of the Torridge Estuary. Behind the seafront, narrow lanes hold shops and pubs, straggling uphill to where the Maritime Museum displays a collection of nautical items. The Visual Arts Festival at the end of May showcases local talent. For the best estuary views, a pint and tasty seafood, head for the two pubs on Irsha Street. ⊗ *Map H2 • Maritime Museum: 01237 422064; open May–Sep 11am–5pm Mon–Fri, 2–5pm Sat & Sun; • adm*

Clovelly

This picturesque settlement clings to a steep cliff and plunges down to a small harbour. The town is privately owned and there is an absence of cars, except for a Land Rover service for visitors who find the

Museum of North Devon

One of Devon's finest museums has a gloriously eclectic collection, including features on the area's wildlife and items relating to the Royal Devon Yeomanry. You can walk through a model Wellington bomber, view fascinating timepieces and admire superbly crafted glassware. A highlight is the Barum Ware – startlingly original pottery for which the area is renowned. ⊗ *Map H2 • The Square, Barnstaple • 01271 346747 • Open 9:30am–5pm Mon–Sat*

Lynton and Lynmouth

These villages on the Exmoor coast, linked by a water-powered funicular, have drawn visitors since the 1800s when the poet Shelley spent his honeymoon here. Nestled among hills, the villages are a haven of tranquillity, though it

---

Tarka the Otter

North Devon's Tarka Line, Tarka Trail and Tarka Country all refer to *Tarka the Otter*, written by Henry Williamson. The book narrates the adventures of a young otter amid the beautiful landscape of North Devon – "the country of the two rivers". The book has retained its place as a classic animal tale, and was made into a film in 1979, narrated by Peter Ustinov.

The River Lyn flowing through Lynmouth

The pannier market, Barnstaple

was not always peaceful here. Lynmouth, by the sea, was devastated by a flash flood in 1952; the Glen Lyn Gorge, through which the torrent raged, holds an exhibition in memory of the event. ◐ *Map J1*

Barnstaple Pannier Market

This covered market in the town centre is the most famous of Devon's "pannier markets" – so called because traders originally brought their wares in baskets or panniers. The markets held here offer antiques, crafts, local produce, household items and clothes. Alongside is Butchers Row, which once held butchers' shops and is now home to a variety of stores.
◐ *Map H2 • Butchers Row, Barnstaple • 01271 379084 • Open: Wed (antiques); Mon & Thu except Jan–Mar (arts and crafts); Tue, Fri & Sat (household items & clothes) • barnstaplepanniermarket.co.uk*

Lundy Island

This remote 5-km- (3-mile-) long sliver of land is located north of Hartland Point. It gets its name from the puffins that inhabit the island (*lunde* is Norse for puffin). Unusual accommodation here includes a lighthouse and a radio room.
◐ *Map G1 • Tourist information: 01271 863636 • www.lundyisland.co.uk*

A Drive along the North Devon Coast

Morning

Begin your tour in the sister villages of **Lynton** and **Lynmouth** at the foot of Exmoor. The upper village, Lynton, is connected by an ingenious cliff railway to Lynmouth. From here it is a short drive to **Ilfracombe**, a cheerfully traditional resort with a bustling harbour. On the coast south of Ilfracombe, the **Woolacombe** and **Croyde** beaches *(see p41)* invite a stopover. Though very different – Croyde is a sheltered inlet while Woolacombe is a long curving bay – both are good for families as well as watersport enthusiasts. You can either indulge in a beachside picnic lunch or drive inland to lunch at the **Broomhill Art Hotel** *(see p71)*. The sculpture garden here will prove absorbing.

Afternoon

In the afternoon, halt at Barnstaple, home to the lively **Pannier Market** as well as the interesting **Museum of Barnstaple and North Devon**. Alternatively, stop at Bideford for a visit to the **Burton Art Gallery and Museum**, which hosts regular exhibitions. Up at the mouth of the estuary, **Appledore** has another museum you can explore, but a stroll along the riverside is equally enjoyable. Proceed west along Bideford Bay to **Clovelly**, an enchanting, well-preserved village and stop for tea. If time allows, take a walk along **Hobby Drive** *(see p36)* or just continue west to **Hartland Abbey** *(see p50)*, a majestic mansion with lovely grounds sweeping down to sea.

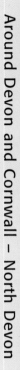

Around Devon and Cornwall – North Devon

Left **Watersmeet near Lynmouth** Right **The harbour at Clovelly**

🔟 Beauty Spots

Valley of the Rocks
West of Lynton, this steep heathland is dominated by rugged rock formations. Herds of wild goats still roam free as they have done here for centuries. ✎ *Map J1*

Watersmeet
In a deep wooded gorge, Hoar Oak Water joins with the River East Lyn on its way down to the sea. Shady riverside walks branch out from here. ✎ *Map J1*

Hartland Point
On Devon's northwestern tip, overlooked by a solitary lighthouse, this remote, storm-battered headland has dramatic coastal views of slate cliffs, jagged black rocks and swirling sea. ✎ *Map G2*

Clovelly
There is no denying the loveliness of this village, with its neat cottages and miniature harbour *(see p68)*.

Saunton Sands
The first view of this 6-km (3-mile) westward-facing strand is breathtaking, with ranks of Atlantic rollers advancing in a stately procession. This spot is a favourite among surfers. ✎ *Map H2*

Lynmouth
The East and West Lyn rivers flow placidly into the sea at this cliff-sheltered Exmoor village.

The Glen Lyn Gorge has woodland walks and waterfalls *(see p68)*.

Northam Burrows
Located next to Westward Ho!, this expanse of grasslands, salt marsh and sand dunes offers wonderful views across the Taw/Torridge Estuary. The broad beach in front attracts surfers and sail-boarders. ✎ *Map H2*

Weare Giffard
This graceful village in the wooded Torridge Valley boasts a 15th-century manor house and a weathered pub. It is accessible from the Tarka Trail. ✎ *Map H2*

Hillsborough
Outside Ilfracombe, the summit of this 136-m (447-ft) hill is one of the few places in the country where you can see the sun rise and set over the sea. ✎ *Map H1*

Lundy Island
This remote outpost where the Atlantic meets the Bristol Channel is either utterly tranquil or in complete uproar, depending on the sea *(see p69)*.

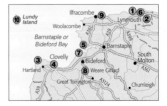

70

Red Lion pub, Clovelly

Price Categories

For a three-course meal for one with half a bottle of wine, including taxes and extra charges.

£	under £20
££	£20–£35
£££	£35–£45
££££	£45–£55
£££££	over £55

☝10 Places to Eat

1 Broomhill Art Hotel
This unusual place houses the relaxed Terra Madre restaurant where the emphasis is on local seasonal produce presented in modern style. Bar meals are also available. ✆ *Map H2 • Muddiford Rd, Barnstaple • 01271 850262 • Open Wed–Sun lunch, Fri & Sat dinner (booking essential Wed, Fri & Sun lunch) • £*

2 The Quay
This fashionable harbourside eatery, co-owned by artist Damien Hirst, features a menu that mixes Mediterranean and British cooking. ✆ *Map H1 • 11 The Quay, Ilfracombe • 01271 868090 • £££*

3 Puffing Billy
The restored waiting room of an old Victorian station serves as a friendly pub and restaurant on the Tarka Trail. Railway memorabilia and two parrots add to the atmosphere. ✆ *Map H2 • Station Hill, Great Torrington • 01805 623050 • Closed evenings Nov–Feb • £*

4 Red Lion
Right on the harbour, this hotel-restaurant offers great views. Local fish and meat dominate the menu. ✆ *Map G2 • Clovelly • 01237 431237 • ££*

5 St Vincent
The Belgian chef of this chic restaurant in a Georgian house serves up an exquisite array of modern European dishes. ✆ *Map J1 • Castle Hill, Lynton • 01598 752244 • Open Wed–Sun evenings • ££*

6 Rising Sun
Right on the harbour, this 14th-century inn claims to have once accommodated the poet Shelley. Enjoy the British-style cuisine in an atmospheric setting. ✆ *Map J1 • Harbourside, Lynmouth • 01598 753223 • £££*

7 Royal George
Boasting splendid estuary views, this traditional pub on a cobbled lane offers bar meals including steak and scampi. ✆ *Map H2 • Irsha St, Appledore • 01237 474335 • ££*

8 Marisco Tavern
Lundy's sole pub is one of the stranger places to have a meal. Granite floors and relics of local shipwrecks set the tone. ✆ *Map G1 • Lundy Island • 01237 431831*

9 Stoke Barton Farm
This tea room in one of Devon's remotest spots provides sustenance in the form of home-made scones and cakes, and has a warm ambience. ✆ *Map G2 • Stoke, Hartland • 01237 441238 • Open Apr–Sep 2–5:30pm Tue–Thu, Sat & Sun*

10 Watersmeet House
At a famous Exmoor beauty spot, this Victorian fishing lodge is now a tea room and garden where you can feast on hearty refreshments before or after exploring the river banks. ✆ *Map J1 • Watersmeet Rd, Lynmouth • 01598 753348 • £*

For more restaurants in the region See pp81, 87, 95 and 103.

71

Left **The Choir, Exeter Cathedral** Right **The Promenade, Plymouth**

South Devon

A GENTEEL AURA PERVADES MUCH OF SOUTH DEVON. *Verdant meadows are interspersed with cob-and-thatch villages and rivers drift serenely through wooded valleys dotted with tidy cottages. Crumbly red cliffs rear above beaches, while in the forbidding expanse of Dartmoor, lonely tors gaze over slopes of bracken and gorse, and isolated communities huddle around centuries-old churches. A world away from these rural scenes are Exeter and Plymouth, the historic power centres, with their scattering of medieval and Elizabethan remains.*

1. Powderham Castle
2. A La Ronde
3. Living Coasts
4. Exeter
5. Church of the Holy Cross
6. Lydford Gorge
7. Plymouth
8. Torre Abbey Mansion
9. Buckland Abbey
10. Dartmoor

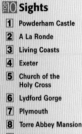

A thatched cottage, Dartmoor National Park

Around Devon and Cornwall – South Devon

Preceding pages **The view from a tor on Dartmoor**

Powderham Castle

Surrounded by a deer park, this stately pile is the long-time seat of the earls of Devon and featured in the film *Remains of the Day*. Tours allow you to view the ornate music room, the majestic dining room, lavish bedrooms and the Victorian kitchen.

Powderham Castle

Kids will love the stories of ghosts, the secret door and the activity trails in the grounds.
* Map K4 • Kenton • 01626 890243
* Open mid-Mar–early Nov: 10am–5:30pm Sun–Fri • Adm • www.powderham.co.uk

A La Ronde

When the Parminter cousins, Jane and Mary, returned from their European travels in 1790, they brought with them trunk-loads of souvenirs and a unique vision. They built this 16-sided house which they filled with their mementos and creations. These ranged from seaweed and sand concoctions to a frieze made of game-bird and chicken feathers, and a shell-covered gallery.
* Map L4 • Summer Lane, Exmouth
* 01395 265514 • Open mid-Mar–early Nov: 11am–5pm Sat–Wed • Adm
* www.nationaltrust.org.uk

The Living Coasts exhibition

Living Coasts

This aquatic exhibition focuses on the coastlines of the world. The reconstructed beaches, cliff faces and an estuary illustrate the diverse wildlife. Spot cormorants, penguins and puffins in an aviary, and South America fur seals in the seal pool. The waterside café offers wonderful views of Tor Bay. Ask about discounted tickets if you are also visiting Paignton Zoo *(see p78)*.
* Map K5 • Beacon Quay, Torquay
* 01803 202470 • Open Apr–Oct: 10am–6pm; Nov–Mar: 10am–4:30pm
* Adm • www.livingcoasts.org.uk

Exeter

Devon's capital is a relaxed place with a historic core that includes the region's oldest cathedral. Other attractions include a network of under-ground passages, historic civic and religious buildings and the old quayside area. The city has an active cultural life, with a year-round programme of festivals and events, and a good selection of theatres and restaurants. With the new Princesshay develop-ment complete, Exeter also offers the region's best shopping opportunities. Enquire at the city's tourist office about walking tours *(see pp18–19)*.

Church of the Holy Cross

This red sandstone structure from around the 15th century is one of Devon's grandest churches. It stands on the site initially occupied by a monastery church, which was founded by the great missionary St Boniface. Born in Crediton around AD 680, he went on to become patron saint of Germany and the Netherlands. Brightly illuminated by large windows, the church building is full of historical interest. Its Lady Chapel is thought to have provided the model for the one in Exeter Cathedral. ✎ *Map K3 • Church St, Crediton • 01363 772669*

Church of the Holy Cross

Lydford Gorge

On the edge of Dartmoor, the River Lyd thunderously gushes through this steep, oak-wooded ravine, home to the spectacular Devil's Cauldron whirlpool and the White Lady Waterfall that plummets 28 m (90 ft). There are walking opportunities along the river and a winding upper path but come prepared with robust boots to navigate the trickier parts. Children must be supervised and access may be difficult for those with mobility problems *(see pp12–13)*.

Plymouth

This historic city, closely associated with Sir Francis Drake, rewards prolonged exploration. Remnants of the Elizabethan city survive, notably in the harbourside Barbican quarter. Other attractions that merit a visit include the beguiling National Marine Aquarium and the Plymouth Gin Distillery. Don't miss the magnificent sea views from Plymouth Hoe, a high grassy esplanade. Bus and walking tours are available all year *(see pp14–15)*.

Torre Abbey Mansion

One of Devon's greatest museums is housed in a mansion house converted from abbey buildings after the Dissolution of the Monasteries in 1539 *(see p34)*. The collection is strong in 19th-century art, including works by Holman Hunt and Burne-Jones. The grounds have medieval ruins and a tithe barn – known as the "Spanish Barn"

White Lady falls, Lydford Gorge

Dartmoor ponies – a mother and her foal

after it was used to hold prisoners from the Spanish Armada. Temporary exhibitions and cultural events are held here. ⊛ Map K5 • King's Drive, Torquay • 01803 293593 • www.torre-abbey.org.uk

Buckland Abbey
The former home of Elizabethan mariners, Richard Grenville and Francis Drake, this handsome manor house is set in beautiful grounds in the Tavy Valley. Visitors can explore the monastic Great Barn, Elizabethan Garden and the Abbey, where galleries feature interactive displays. Exhibits include Drake's Drum which, according to legend, will sound when England is in danger to summon Drake from his grave. ⊛ Map H5 • Yelverton • 01822 853607 • Open mid-Feb–mid-Mar: 2–5pm weekends; mid-Mar–Oct: 10:30am–5:30pm Fri–Wed; early Nov–late Dec: noon–4pm Fri–Sun • Adm • www.nationaltrust.org.uk

Dartmoor
In a region dominated by the sea, Dartmoor is a windy wasteland where semi-wild ponies roam. Many prehistoric remains lie scattered across the moor, while on its edges are market towns, Okehampton and Tavistock. This area demands active exploration with opportunities for caving, walking, canoeing and wildlife watching. (see pp12–13).

A Driving Tour in South Devon

Morning

🕐 Start from the fishing village of **Beer** (see p79), associated with the infamous exploits of smuggler Jack Rattenbury, located close to the Dorset border. You can grab a crab sandwich on the beach. Follow the A3052 east to **Sidmouth** (see p79), whose seafront and Esplanade are ideal for a stroll. The town is studded with well-preserved villas from the Regency period. The museum here includes a lovely display of lace. Indulge in some good seaside lunch at Sidmouth.

Afternoon

Further west, just outside **Exmouth** (see p79) off the A376, stop to admire **A La Ronde** (see p75), a remarkable 16-sided folly constructed by cousins Jane and Mary Parminter. Continue to the M5, then take the A380 and A381 south to **Totnes** (see p79). Despite its hippy vibe, the town retains much of its Elizabethan character and has a Norman castle and a 14th-century church. The town's tearooms offer tasty refreshments. From Totnes, drive or take a river cruise down the River Dart to the sailing resort of **Dartmouth** (see p79), also filled with mementos from the Elizabethan era. From Totnes or Dartmouth, it is an easy excursion to the South Hams, an area of sleepy villages and soothing views. Unless you are based in Totnes or Dartmouth, either stay over in Kingsbridge or Salcombe, or head back up the A381 to **Exeter** (see pp18–19).

Visitors arriving by cycle or public transport to the Lydford Gorge and Buckland Abbey get discounts on the admission price.

Left **Fairlynch Museum** Right **Bicton Park**

🔟 Best of the Rest

1 Fairlynch Museum
This 19-century *cottage orné* houses a collection of local memorabilia including lace, costumes and toys. ⊗ *Map L4 • 27 Fore St, Budleigh Salterton • 1395 442666 • Open Apr–Sep: 2–4:30pm • Adm*

2 Beer Quarry Caves
These caves have been in use since Roman times for quarrying Beer stone. ⊗ *Map M4 • Quarry Lane, Beer • 01297 625830 • Open mid-Mar–Oct: 10am–5:30pm • Adm • www.beerquarrycaves.com*

3 Burgh Island
This tiny isle can be reached in high tide by sea tractor. Once there, you can stay in the luxurious Burgh Island Hotel *(see p114)*. ⊗ *Map J6 • Bigbury-on-Sea*

4 Overbeck's Museum
A quirky collection gathered by inventor Otto Overbeck is housed in this museum. ⊗ *Map J6 • Sharpitor, Salcombe • 01548 842893 • Times vary • Adm • www.nationaltrust. org.uk*

5 Paignton Zoo
This zoo is designed to mimic the natural habitats of the animals that live here. ⊗ *Map K5 • Totnes Rd, Paignton • 01803 697500 • Open 10am–6pm (closes 5pm in winter) • Adm • www.paigntonzoo.org.uk*

6 Bicton Park
This horticultural idyll includes a formal garden repu-tedly inspired by Versailles in the 1730s and a Palm House from the 1820s. ⊗ *Map L4 • East Budleigh, Budleigh Salterton • 01395 568465 • Open summer: 10am–6pm; winter: closes 5pm • Adm • www.bictongardens.co.uk*

7 Allhallows Museum
Housed in the oldest build-ing in town, this museum dis-plays fine lace. ⊗ *Map L3 • High St, Honiton • 01404 44966 • Times vary • Adm • www.honitonmuseum.co.uk*

8 Cookworthy Museum of Rural Life
The museum is named after the pioneer of hard-paste English porcelain made from China Clay. ⊗ *Map J6 • 108 Fore St, Kingsbridge • 01548 853235 • Times vary • Adm*

9 Berry Head, Torbay
This site is home to guillemots and the endangered Greater Horseshoe Bat. ⊗ *Map K5*

10 Blackpool Sands
This is one of South Devon's premier beaches, home to the renowned Venus Café. ⊗ *Map K6 • Near Dartmouth • www.blackpoolsands. co.uk*

Unless otherwise stated, the museums all close in winter.

Left **Sidmouth** Centre **Glassware at Cider Press, Totnes** Right **Boats at Budleigh Salterton**

🔟 Towns and Villages

Salcombe
At the mouth of the placid Kingsbridge Estuary, Devon's southernmost port is a magnet for sailors. Beaches, coastal walks and Overbeck's Museum are all nearby. ✎ *MapJ6*

Sidmouth
The queen of East Devon resorts, elegant Sidmouth has a long Esplanade fronted by a shingle strand, though families prefer Jacob's Ladder, a more secluded beach to the west. ✎ *Map L4*

Totnes
The age of this riverside town is attested by its Norman castle and medieval remains. It is popular with craftworkers and has some fine glassware ✎ *Map K5*

Cockington
There is no denying the rustic appeal of this well-preserved village, a calm contrast to the ebullience of neighbouring Torquay. ✎ *Map K5*

Brixham
Much of the seafood served in the region's restaurants is landed at this harbour. A replica of the *Golden Hind*, the vessel in which Francis Drake circumnavigated the globe, is moored here. ✎ *Map K5*

Beer
The village is best known for fishing, smuggling and Beer stone, a prized building material. A culvert carries a stream along the main street, from where you descend to the beach. ✎ *Map M4*

Dartmouth
The Royal Regatta and the Royal Naval College confirm this port's yachting credentials. Impressive Tudor buildings and a castle add to its allure. ✎ *Map K6*

Budleigh Salterton
John Millais painted his famous *Boyhood of Raleigh* on the pebble beach of this village. The Fairlynch Museum here is well worth a wander. ✎ *Map L4*

Exmouth
Primarily a family resort, Exmouth gets quite lively during the summer. The Beacon, an elegant row overlooking the sea, once accommodated the wives of Byron and Nelson. ✎ *Map K4*

Torquay
Capital of the so-called English Riviera, engaging Torquay, with its palms and fairy lights, smacks unmistakably of the Mediterranean. ✎ *Map K5*

Left **St Mary's** Centre **South Devon Railway** Right **Buckfast Abbey**

Sights Along the River Dart

1 Buckfast Abbey
The River Dart flows out of Dartmoor through the grounds of this Benedictine house. The few monks still living here are famed for their tonic wine. ✎ *Map H5 • Buckfastleigh • 01364 645550 • Open 9am–6pm Mon–Thu & Sat, (10am Fri), noon–6pm Sun • www.buckfast.org.uk*

2 Elizabethan Museum
This museum in a cloth merchant's home was built in 1575 and has a room devoted to Totnes-born mathematician Charles Babbage, who built the forerunner of the computer. ✎ *Map K5 • 70 Fore St, Totnes • 01803 863821 • Open mid-Mar–Oct: 10:30am–5pm Mon–Fri • Adm*

3 St Mary's
This red sandstone building boasts a rood-screen of delicate tracery dating from 1460. ✎ *Map K5 • 61 Fore St, Totnes • 01803 867011*

4 The Guildhall
Built on the ruins of a priory in 1553, Guildhall later housed a courtroom and jail cells. It displays a table used by Oliver Cromwell (*see p18*).

5 South Devon Railway
Travel back in time in this Great Western Railway coach hauled by a steam locomotive. The line follows the Dart between Totnes and Buckfastleigh. ✎ *Map J5 • Station Rd, Buckfastleigh • 08453 451420 • Open Apr–Oct • Adm • www.southdevonrailway.org*

6 Riverlink Cruises
The most relaxing way to explore the Dart is a cruise between Totnes and Dartmouth, which takes about an hour. ✎ *Map K5 • 5 Lower St, Dartmouth • 01803 834488 • Times vary due to the tide • Adm • www.riverlink.co.uk*

7 Greenway
This riverside estate was the birthplace of Elizabethan adventurer Humphrey Gilbert and later the residence of Agatha Christie. The Barn Gallery and gardens are open to visitors. ✎ *Map J6 • Galmpton, Devon • 01803 842382 • Open Mar–Oct: 10:30am–5pm Wed–Sun • Adm • www.nationaltrust.org.uk*

8 Dartmouth Museum
An absorbing collection of maritime models and other items relating to Dartmouth are housed in this merchant's house. ✎ *Map K5 • Duke St, Dartmouth • 01803 832923 • Open Apr–Oct: 10am–4pm Mon–Sat; Nov–Mar: noon–3pm Mon–Sat • Adm*

9 Dartmouth Royal Regatta
Pomp and pageantry are the order of the day at this annual jamboree celebrating the port's maritime traditions. ✎ *Map K5 • 01803 834912 (Regatta period only) • Aug end • www.dartmouthregatta.co.uk*

10 Dartington Hall
Founded by US heiress Dorothy Elmhirst, this arts and education centre hosts a range of cultural events. ✎ *Map J5 • 01803 847070 • www.dartington.org*

Price Categories

For a three course	£	under £20
meal for one with half	££	£20–£35
a bottle of wine (or	£££	£35–£45
equivalent meal), taxes	££££	£45–£55
and extra charges.	£££££	over £55

Left **Michael Caines at Abode** Right **Horn of Plenty**

Places to Eat

Horn of Plenty
This Georgian house in the Tamar Valley serves creative British cuisine. Monday's pot-luck menu is cheaper but offers less choice, though the quality is guaranteed. ◎ *Map H4 • Gulworthy, Dartmoor • 01822 832528 • ££££*

Gidleigh Park
Noted chef Michael Caines has garnered two Michelin stars for his original interpretations of modern European cuisine at this luxurious hotel-restaurant. Reservations are essential. ◎ *Map J4 • Chagford • 01647 432367 • £££££*

Dartmoor Inn
Indulge in imaginatively prepared Mediterranean and British dishes at this gastro-pub. The cosy dining areas have open fires and wood or stone floors. ◎ *Map H4 • Lydford • 01822 820221 • Closed Mon lunch & Sun dinner • £££*

Michael Caines at Abode
This spacious restaurant is a good setting for the culinary creations of master-chef Michael Caines. The set-price lunches are particularly good value. ◎ *Map P2 • Cathedral Yard, Exeter • 01392 223638 • Closed Sun • £££££*

Barrel o' Beer
This pub offers whatever the fishing boats have brought in that day, plus some meat and seafood dishes. ◎ *Map M4 • Fore St, Beer • 01297 20099 • Closed Wed & Sun in winter • ££*

Burton Farmhouse
This restaurant makes good use of local and seasonal produce to dish out wholesome fare. A secluded patio is well-suited to summer dining. ◎ *Map K5 • Galmpton • 01548 561210 • Closed Mon–Sat lunch • £££*

22 Mill Street
Hidden away in a tranquil Dartmoor village, 22 Mill Street has an upmarket feel and a modern European menu. It is worth a detour. ◎ *Map J4 • 22 Mill St, Chagford • 01647 432244 • £££*

Barbican Kitchen
Set in an historic Barbican building, this relaxed brasserie attracts shoppers at lunchtime and romantic couples in the evening. ◎ *Map Q6 • 58 Southside St, Plymouth • 01752 604448 • £££*

Tanners
Fine food and wine can be enjoyed in one of Plymouth's oldest buildings. The set-price menus at Tanners feature poultry, game and fresh seafood. ◎ *Map P5 • Prysten House, Finewell St, Plymouth • 01752 252001 • Closed Sun & Mon • ££££*

Café Alf Resco
A local breakfast and coffee favourite, this child-friendly café with a terrace serves pastries, baguettes, and lunchtime specials. ◎ *Map K5 • Lower Street, Dartmouth • 01803 835880 • Closed for lunch except in summer • No credit cards • £*

Unless otherwise stated, all restaurants accept credit cards and serve vegetarian meals.

Left **Tintagel Castle** Right **Newquay Zoo**

North Cornwall

WITH THE ATLANTIC HAMMERING ON THE COAST, *much of North Cornwall has a harsh feel in contrast with the more sheltered character of Cornwall's southern seaboard. Abandoned engine houses and chimney stacks recall its industrial past, while numerous Wesleyan chapels are testament to the faith of its mining population. Between the cliffs are some of the region's best surf beaches. You can indulge in the county's finest seafood in Padstow, explore architectural styles at Prideaux Place and Lanhydrock, and enjoy the peace of the Camel Estuary. The area is rich in Arthurian connections, not least the ruins of Tintagel Castle and sites on Bodmin Moor.*

Left **The harbour at Boscastle** Right **Rick Stein's Café, Padstow**

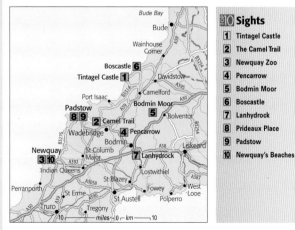

Sights

1. **Tintagel Castle**
2. **The Camel Trail**
3. **Newquay Zoo**
4. **Pencarrow**
5. **Bodmin Moor**
6. **Boscastle**
7. **Lanhydrock**
8. **Prideaux Place**
9. **Padstow**
10. **Newquay's Beaches**

Tintagel Castle

This coastal stronghold is one of the country's most romantic castle ruins. Its appeal is also due to its Arthurian associations, as the supposed birthplace of the Once and Future King. The structure though, probably dates from the 12th century, when it belonged to the Norman earls of Cornwall. There may already have been a Roman fortification and traces of a Celtic monastery have been found. Whatever the story, it is highly atmospheric and on a dramatic site. *Map D2 • Tintagel • 01840 770328 • Open Apr–Sep: 10am–6pm; Oct: 10am–5pm; Nov–Mar: 10am–4pm • Adm • www.english-heritage.org.uk*

The Camel Trail

This walking and cycling route runs for 27 km (17 miles) between Padstow and the edge of Bodmin Moor. The Padstow–Wadebridge section is on a resurfaced railway track and offers glimpses of the abundant birdlife along the Camel Estuary. From Wadebridge, the route heads southeast towards Bodmin before following the winding river through tranquil woods north to Poley's Bridge. Tourist offices at Padstow, Wadebridge and Bodmin have leaflets, detailed guides and maps. *Map D3*

Newquay Zoo

More than 130 species are held in such enclosures as the Penguin Pool, Monkey Walk, African Plains and Wildlife at Night. The zoo has an active conservation and education agenda. Visitors can meet the animals, watch them being fed and get lost in the Dragon Maze. Look out for the graceful Red Pandas and comical Ruffed Lemurs, and the African lions that feed from meat contained in papier-maché zebras. *Map C4 • Trenance Gardens, Newquay • 01637 873342 • Open Apr–Sep: 9:30am–6pm; Oct–Mar: 10am–5pm • Adm • www.newquayzoo.org.uk*

Pencarrow

Inhabited by a branch of one of Cornwall's most powerful old families, this elegant Georgian house was constructed in the 1760s and stands at the end of a mile-long drive. The interior boasts an arched inner hall filled with dolls and pushchairs, a music room with an exquisite Rococo ceiling and paintings by Reynolds. Outside are extensive formal and wooded gardens, designed in the 19th century by the Radical politician, Sir William Molesworth. *Map D3 • Bodmin • 01208 841369 • Open late Mar–mid-Oct: 11am–5pm Sun–Thu • Adm • www.pencarrow.co.uk*

Pencarrow House

Share your travel recommendations on **traveldk.com**

Cornwall's Mineworks

An iconic image of the Cornish landscape is the engine house and chimney that denotes the existence of a former mine. North Cornwall is dotted with these castle-like granite structures. They hark back to a time when the county was producing up to two thirds of the world's total output of copper and tin. The industry fell into decline in the 1870s.

Bodmin Moor

Cornwall's great inland wilderness is made of the same granite mass as Dartmoor and has the same mixture of rugged grandeur interspersed with splashing rivers and shady woodland. Dotted with mysterious prehistoric remains such as the Hurlers and Trethevy Quoit, the moor has a plethora of places associated with King Arthur and his knights. In the midst of the desolate expanses lie appealing villages, such as Blisland, St Neot's and Altarnun. ◈ Map E3

Boscastle

The great wall of cliffs, making up much of North Cornwall's coast is sliced through by the Valency and Jordan rivers here, which twist through a ravine to a tiny harbour. The village was devastated by a flash flood in 2004, but the damage has been repaired and Boscastle has reverted to its natural serenity. Look out for the famous blowhole known as Devil's Bellows, below Penally Point. ◈ Map D2

Lanhydrock

The finest house in Cornwall is a must-see. Originally Jacobean, little of the original construction survived a fire in 1881, but the Victorian interior visible today makes up for the loss, lovingly restored by the National Trust. The 50-odd rooms include the rather cramped maids' bedrooms and the lavish quarters of the Agar-Robartes family, but the highlights are the impressive kitchens and sculleries. Huge gardens and wooded parkland are wonderful and worth exploring *(see pp8–9)*.

Prideaux Place

This historic mansion blends Elizabethan splendour with 18th-century Gothic decor. Highlights include the Great Chamber, with biblical tales illustrated on the plaster ceiling, and the oak-panelled Great Hall, now a dining room, showing a frieze of small animals. Look out for the carving of Elizabeth I

Golitha Falls on the Fowey River, Bodmin Moor

Prideaux Place

standing on a pig (a symbol of vice) next to the fireplace. The morning room has paintings by the Cornish portrait artist John Opie *(see p30)*.

Padstow

Both fishing port and seaside resort, Padstow has developed a profile in recent years as Cornwall's gastronomic capital. Ever since seafood champion Rick Stein established a restaurant here in the 1970s, the town has become synonymous with gourmet food. The premier beaches nearby attract surfers and families. The May Day Obby Oss festivities are among the country's most theatrical and the sheltered Camel Estuary boasts great walking and cycling routes *(see pp30–31)*.

Newquay's Beaches

After the arrival of the railway in the 1870s, Newquay developed as a beach resort. In recent years, it has become Britain's pre-eminent surf resort with competitions held at Fistral Beach. Holywell Bay and Perran Beach are also highly regarded, while the more sheltered Towan Beach, Tolcarne and Lusty Glaze are suitable for families. Watergate Bay attracts the extreme sports crowd. ◈ *Map C4*

A Drive Along Cornwall's Northern Coast

Morning

Cornwall's northernmost resort of **Bude** has fine beaches for a morning dip. From here, the A39 plunges south; branch off onto the B3263 to **Boscastle** for a stroll along its harbour, which has a **Museum of Witchcraft**. On the way in or out of the village, stop at St Juliot's Church, where Thomas Hardy once worked as an architect. Six km (4 miles) west is **Tintagel** *(see p83)*, one of Cornwall's popular sights on account of its ruined castle said to have been Arthur's birthplace. After touring the castle, lunch in a local café, or escape the crowds by heading south to the harbour village of **Port Isaac** *(see p86)*.

Afternoon

After lunch, head inland to **Bodmin**, an ancient market town featuring Cornwall's largest parish church. You can also visit the **Bodmin Jail** *(see p86)* and the Courtroom Experience next to the tourist office, where you can cast your vote in a re-enactment of a celebrated murder trial of 1844. From **Bodmin**, take the A30 west to **Newquay** which has some of Cornwall's best beaches. The county's only zoo is located here. Head up the coast on the B3276 and stop at **Watergate Bay** *(see p41)*, where the **Beach Hut** *(see p87)* is a great spot for snacks. Surfing equipment can be hired from the **Extreme Academy**. Continue up the B3276 to **Padstow** and dine at one of its seafood restaurants.

Left **Port Isaac** Right **Cardinham Woods**

🔟 Best of the Rest

1 Trerice
This Elizabethan manor has a splendid barrel-roofed Great Chamber. You can play kayles (Cornish skittles) in the grounds. ⊗ *Map C4 • Kestle Mill, Newquay • 01637 875404 • Open mid-Mar–early Nov: 11am–5pm Sun–Fri • Adm*

2 Port Isaac
A typical North Cornish fishing village with winding lanes and a working harbour. The surrounding cliffs offer fine walking. ⊗ *Map D3*

3 Tintagel Old Post Office
This 14th-century manor house is furnished with local oak pieces. ⊗ *Map D3 • Fore St, Tintagel • 01840 770024 • Open Mar–Sep 11am–5pm daily; Oct 11am–4pm daily • Adm*

4 Bedruthan Steps
The jagged slate outcrops on this beach were supposed to be the stepping stones of the giant Bedruthan. A cliffside staircase descends to the beach but bathing is unsafe. ⊗ *Map C3*

5 Cardinham Woods
There are four forest walks and a waymarked trail for mountain-bikers in these woods. ⊗ *Map E3 • Bikes available for hire*

6 Blue Reef Aquarium
Get close to everything from sea horses to octopus in this aquarium near Newquay harbour. ⊗ *Map C4 • Towan Promenade, Newquay • 01637 878134 • 10am–5pm daily • Adm*

7 Bodmin Jail
Built in 1779, this former jail is a fascinating attraction, with tours of the cells, visits to the "execution pit" and a ghost walk offered to visitors. ⊗ *Map D4 • Berrycombe Rd, Bodmin • 01208 76292 • Open 10am daily • Adm*

8 St Enodoc
This tiny 13th-century church appears buried amid dunes in the middle of a golf course. Poet John Betjeman is buried here. ⊗ *Map D3 • St Minver • 01208 862398*

9 Crackington Haven
This highly scenic beach is backed by dramatic cliffs rising to 130 m (430 ft), with strangely contorted rock strata. ⊗ *Map E2*

10 Cornish Mines and Engines
Two great beam engines are preserved in their engine houses at this museum. ⊗ *Map C5 • Pool, Redruth • 01209 315027 • Open Mar–Oct 11am–5pm Sun, Mon & Wed–Fri • Adm*

Price Categories

For a three-course meal for one with half a bottle of wine, including taxes and extra charges.	£ under £20
	££ £20–£35
	£££ £35–£45
	££££ £45–£55
	£££££ over £55

Rick Stein's flagship Seafood Restaurant

TOP 10 Places to Eat

1 Seafood Restaurant
The flagship of Rick Stein's culinary empire offers a range of fish dishes from cod, chips and peas to monkfish vindaloo and lobster thermidor. Booking is essential. ® Map D3 • Riverside, Padstow • 01841 532700 • £££££

2 St Petroc's Bistro
Smaller than the Seafood Restaurant, this Stein venture has fewer choices on the menu and lower prices, but delivers the goods. Meat gets equal billing with seafood. ® Map D3 • 4 New St, Padstow • 01841 532700 • £££

3 No. 6
Dress up for dining in this Georgian town house with contemporary decor and sophisticated food. ® Map D3 • 6 Middle St, Padstow • 01841 532093 • ££££

4 Fifteen
A bevy of young chefs demonstrate their culinary expertise in Jamie Oliver's restaurant in a fantastic location overlooking the beach. Food has a strong Italian stamp and the style is casual-chic. ® Map C4 • Watergate Bay • 01637 861000 • ££££

5 Blisland Inn
This village-green pub off Bodmin Moor serves real ales and food ranging from bar snacks to rib-eye steak. There is a family room and outdoor tables. ® Map E3 • Blisland • 01208 850739 • ££

6 Stein's Fish & Chips
The most reasonable and relaxed of Stein's eateries, this place has some of the most succulent fish and chips in the West Country. ® Map D3 • South Quay, Padstow • 01841 532700 • £

7 Rick Stein's Café
This place has a Continental feel and is great for breakfast, coffee or a full meal. Dishes include Thai fish cakes and mussels with crème fraiche. ® Map D3 • 10 Middle St, Padstow • 01841 532700 • ££

8 Life's a Beach
This restaurant is located right on the beach. By day, it serves baguettes, burgers and ice cream, and transforms into a fancy restaurant serving British and European dishes in the evening. ® Map E2 • Summerleaze Beach, Bude • 01288 355222 • £££

9 The Chy
This cool and contemporary bar-restaurant offers salads and burgers by day, and steaks and seafood in the evening. DJs play at weekends. ® Map C4 • 12 Beach Rd, Newquay • 01637 873415 • £££

10 The Beach Hut
With the same stunning beachside location as Fifteen, this is a funkier, more casual place for snacks or evening meals in summer. Fish pie and chicken satay are on the menu. ® Map C4 • Watergate Bay • 01637 860877 • ££

Left **A boatyard on the River Fal, Roseland Peninsula** Right **Royal Cornwall Museum**

South Cornwall

WITH ITS INDENTED COASTLINE AND NUMEROUS RIVER ESTUARIES interspersed with secluded settlements, this is a region of unexpected surprises. The charms of Fowey and fishing villages such as Polperro and Mevagissey should not be missed. Cornwall's capital, Truro, is small enough to negotiate easily on foot. Its cathedral and the Royal Cornwall Museum are the main sights here. The most famous attraction however, is the Eden Project, a high-tech garden for the third millennium. South Cornwall's other major gardens, Trelissick and Heligan, are must-sees for plant fans, while south of here, the picturesque Roseland Peninsula is good for exploring.

Sights

1. Eden Project
2. Lost Gardens of Heligan
3. Roseland Peninsula
4. Royal Cornwall Museum
5. Polperro
6. St Mawes Castle
7. Fowey
8. Truro Cathedral
9. Trelissick Garden
10. Cotehele House

A view of the River Fowey from Saints' Way

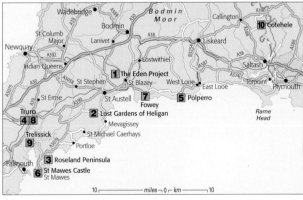

Preceding pages **St Michael's Mount**

Eden Project

Eden Project
Since opening in a former clay pit in 2000, this has become one of Cornwall's success stories. With its giant greenhouses and imaginative scope, Eden is much more than just an upmarket theme park. Rather, it describes itself as a "living theatre of plants and people" – a fantastic illustration of the diversity of the earth's plant life. Above all, the striking beauty of these plants make this an essential stop and one worth visiting at different times of the year in order to capture its seasonal changes (see pp10–11).

Lost Gardens of Heligan
"Lost" for 70 years and neglected for even longer, this salvaged Victorian garden is a triumph of horticultural skill. Presenting a splendid pageantry of plants in diverse habitats including ferneries, fruit houses, Italian gardens and a productive Kitchen Garden, this subtropical "Jungle" and "Lost Valley" will appeal to both adults and kids. There is a strong emphasis on conservation and indoor plasma screens allow visitors to observe the wildlife at close quarters. ◈ Map D4 • Pentewan, St Austell • 01726 845100 • Open Mar–Oct: 10am–6pm daily; Nov–Feb: 10am–5pm daily • Adm • www.heligan.com

Roseland Peninsula
A sleepy backwater planted with lush palms and subtropical vegetation, Roseland Peninsula is edged by low cliffs with fine sea views from St Anthony's Head. There are idyllic creeks and sheltered beaches to explore, as well as sailing boats and kayaks to hire. The secluded churches of St Just-in-Roseland and St Anthony-in-Roseland are also worth viewing. The peninsula can be comfortably toured by bicycle, and may be reached via the year-round Falmouth–St Mawes passenger ferry. From St Mawes, a summer ferry crosses to Place, not far from St Anthony Head. ◈ Map C5

Royal Cornwall Museum
This museum is a cornucopia of Cornish culture, embracing everything from Bronze Age pottery to Newlyn art. The minerals display, based on a collection made 200 years ago, is of international significance. You can also admire the impressive collection of fossils. Botanical and zoological specimens are beautifully represented by items as diverse as stuffed puffins, butterflies, shells and pressed plants. Regular and varied exhibitions are held here. ◈ Map C5 • River Street, Truro • 01872 272205 • Open 10am–4:45pm Mon–Sat

Lost Gardens of Heligan

The China Clay Story

No one passing through the St Austell area can fail to notice the vast conical spoil heaps linked to the local China Clay industry. The substance is used in a variety of products, from paint and paper to medicines. You can learn about its history and applications at the fascinating China Clay Country Park *(see p94)*.

The fishing village of Polperro

5 Polperro

At peak times, this classic Cornish fishing village gets rather too commercialized and crowded, but visit out of season, or step out early in the morning, and you can appreciate its authentic charm. A long main street, mostly traffic-free, leads down alongside a stream and quaint cottages to a huddle of houses around the harbour. An old pilchard factory holds an absorbing Smuggling and Fishing Museum. ◈ *Map E4*

6 St Mawes Castle

Though the lesser of the two 16th-century artillery forts at the mouth of the Carrick Roads Estuary (the other is Pendennis), this castle is better preserved and sports heraldic devices and Latin inscriptions dedicated to Henry VIII and Edward VI. The interior has living quarters and gun rooms displaying ships' cannons from the 1800s, and an impressive bronze "saker" cannon of about 1560, cast by Venetian gunmaster Alberghetti and recovered from the sea off the Devon coast. ◈ *Map C5 • St Mawes • 01326 270526 • Open late Mar–Jun & Sep: 10am–5pm; Jul & Aug: 10am–6pm; Oct: 10am–4pm daily; Nov–Mar: 10am–4pm Fri–Mon • Adm*

7 Fowey

Climbing up the west bank of the River Fowey, this was one of the foremost ports of medieval England and is still a busy harbour town. Most of the maritime activity, however, is now to do with pleasure boats anchored in the estuary. It is worth hiring a boat to enjoy the beauty of the river. ◈ *Map E4*

8 Truro Cathedral

Cornwall's capital is over-shadowed by the soaring spires of its cathedral, a neo-Gothic confection completed in 1910. The faux-medieval style is the cause of much debate in this predominantly Georgian city, but there is no denying the impact of its impressive interior. The Robartes Memorial, showing effigies of a merchant and his wife propped up on their elbows, is one of the eye-catching monuments within. Free guided tours are offered in summer. ◈ *Map C5 • St Mary's St, Truro • 01872 276782*

St Mawes Castle

Trelissick Garden

This lovely, extensive garden has lawns, flowerbeds and hollows filled with rare plants and shrubs, sprawling parkland and miles of woodland paths with panoramic views of the River Fal. Late April, early May and September are the best times to visit, though there is always something to see. A gallery shows Cornish craftwork.
🔦 Map C5 • Feock • 01872 862090 • Open Feb–Oct: 10:30am–5:30pm daily; Nov–Jan: 11am–4pm • Adm

Cotehele House

The excellent condition of this Tudor abode is due to its abandonment by its owners, the Edgcumbe family, who left it intact for a more accessible home outside Plymouth (see pp14–15). It remained with the family until the National Trust took over in 1947. The house has original furniture, armour and a collection of embroideries and tapestries, best seen on a bright day as the rooms have no electric light. 🔦 Map F3 • St Dominick, Saltash • 01579 351346 • Open mid-Mar–early Nov: 11am–4:30pm Sat–Thu • Adm

Truro Cathedral

A Driving Tour in South Cornwall

Morning

Start your journey in **Looe**, a traditional resort that has gained reputation as a shark-fishing centre in recent years. A 6-km (4-mile) drive from here takes you to **Polperro**, whose tightly packed houses and minuscule harbour are best appreciated before the crowds arrive. There is a small smuggling and fishing museum here. From **Polperro**, a scenic minor road leads west to Bodinnick village, where regular ferries cross to **Fowey**. It has a good selection of pubs and bistros that would make suitable lunch stops (there is a car park near the ferry quay). Before or after eating, take a stroll around **Fowey**, to see **St Catherine's Castle**, one of Henry VIII's fortifications, or, follow the **Hall Walk** (see p36).

Afternoon

From **Fowey**, take the A3082 to **St Austell**, from which the A390, B3287 and A3078 will bring you to **St Mawes** on the Carrick Roads Estuary. Here, a large Henrician castle offers views over the river. If you have time, explore the **Roseland Peninsula** (see p91), an area of backwaters and churches. North of St Mawes, **Trelissick Garden** offers captivating woodland walks. The King Harry ferry crosses the river, from where it is a short drive to the county capital, **Truro**. Dominated by its neo-Gothic cathedral and an excellent museum, this relaxed city has a good choice of restaurants and accommodation.

Left **Titanic display at the Shipwreck and Heritage Centre** Right **The ruins of Restormel Castle**

Best of the Rest

1 Shipwreck and Heritage Centre

This collection holds discoveries from over 150 shipwrecks, including memorabilia from the *Titanic* – both the film and the wreck. ◈ *Map D4 • Quay Rd, Charlestown • 01726 69897 • Open Mar–Oct: 10am–5pm daily • Adm • www.shipwreckcharlestown.com*

2 Restormel Castle

This excellent example of a circular shell keep dates from the 13th century. The parapet offers marvellous views over the Fowey Valley. ◈ *Map E4 • Lostwithiel • 01208 872687 • Opening times vary • Adm • www.english-heritage.org.uk*

3 Veryan

Close to good beaches, Veryan is known for its 200-year-old circular houses designed to prevent the devil from hiding in corners. ◈ *Map D5*

4 Mount Edgcumbe

Rebuilt after World War II, this 16th-century house has fine displays of Chinese porcelain and Flemish tapestries *(see p14)*.

5 Carrick Roads Estuary

This estuary complex is one of the world's largest natural harbours. It has lovely coastal walks and sandy coves. ◈ *Map C5*

6 Mevagissey

With its long tradition of fishing and smuggling, this busy port is worth visiting for its museum, pubs and seafood. ◈ *Map D5*

7 King Harry Ferry

Vehicles travelling between St Mawes and Falmouth can save several miles by taking this chain-driven ferry across the Fal, in operation here since 1888. ◈ *Map C5 • Feock, Truro • 01872 863132 • www.kingharryscornwall.co.uk*

8 Caerhays Castle

Take a guided tour of this 19th-century castle that forms an elegant backdrop to Porthluney Cove beach. ◈ *Map D5 • Gorran, St Austell • 01872 501310 • Open Mar–May: tours noon–3pm Mon–Fri • Adm • www.caerhays.co.uk*

9 China Clay Country Park

This place provides a fascinating insight into the China Clay industry, with interactive displays projecting local history. Nature trails are also organized here. ◈ *Map D4 • Wheal Martyn, St Austell • 01726 850362 • Times vary • Adm • www.wheal-martyn.com*

10 Castle Dore

This Iron Age hillfort, with concentric rings of defensive ridges, is considered the palace of the legendary King Mark of Cornwall. ◈ *Map E4 • Golant*

Price Categories

For a three-course	£ under £20
meal for one with	££ £20–£35
half a bottle of wine,	£££ £35–£45
including taxes and	££££ £45–£55
extra charges.	£££££ over £55

The terrace at Hotel Tresanton

Places to Eat

1 One Eyed Cat
A church converted into a cool eatery where you can snack on tapas, sup on seafood or have a drink. There are DJs at weekends and occasional live bands. ✪ Map C5 • 16 Kenwyn St, Truro • 01872 222122 • £££

2 Sam's
A buzzy place with a rock 'n' roll feel. The menu here includes salads, burgers, grills and fish bouillabaisse. Queues form at busy times (no reservations). ✪ Map E4 • 20 Fore St, Fowey • 01726 832273 • ££

3 Driftwood Restaurant
Fresh seafood and local meat dishes are the mainstays of the menu at this elegant hotel-restaurant perched above the sea, offering fine views. ✪ Map C5 • Rosevine, Portscatho • 01872 580644 • Open only for dinner daily • £££££

4 Eden Project
Local, seasonal ingredients are used at the restaurants at the Eden site, offering vegetarian, vegan and gluten-free options (see p11).

5 Alvorada
For a break from West Country food, try this Portuguese place, a few minutes from the harbour. Local seafood is strong on the menu, with speciality items from Portugal. ✪ Map D5 • 2 Polkirt Hill, Mevagissey • 01726 842055 • Times vary in winter • ££

6 The Other Place
Fresh fish and shellfish are the main event in this elegant dining space. There's also a take-away counter for burgers and ice creams. ✪ Map E4 • 41 Fore St, Fowey • 01726 833636 • Times vary in winter • £££

7 Saffron
This friendly bistro offers grilled seafood, meat and organic beer. Express lunches and early-evening menus are good value. ✪ Map C5 • 5 Quay St, Truro • 01872 263771 • Opening times vary • ££

8 Hotel Tresanton
Modern Mediterranean food is served in this hotel overlooking the sea. A terrace offers alfresco dining. ✪ Map C5 • 27 Lower Castle Rd, St Mawes • 01326 270055 • ££££

9 Q
This restaurant at the Old Quay House Hotel (see p116), enjoys splendid views over the River Fowey and immaculate food to match. ✪ Map E4 • Old Quay House Hotel, 28 Fore St, Fowey • 01726 833302 • Apr–May no lunch Tue; Oct–Apr no lunch • £££

10 Charlotte's Victorian Tea House
This restored tea house serves sandwiches and hot snacks, but is best-known for home-made cakes and cream teas. ✪ Map C5 • 1 Boscawen St, Truro • 01872 263706 • Open 10am–5pm Mon–Sat • £

Left **Cliffs at Land's End** Right **Penlee House in Penzance**

West Cornwall and the Isles of Scilly

FOR MANY, THE WESTERN END OF CORNWALL – and of Britain – is the quintessence of everything that makes the county special. Here, you will find every kind of landscape and settlement that Cornwall has to offer, from the sailing port of Falmouth to the fishing hamlet of Mousehole, from the bare moorland of the Penwith peninsula to the sandy Whitesand Bay, and from the creeks of the River Helford to the inhospitable cliffs at Zennor. Poke around the region's numerous prehistoric remains and explore the island stronghold of St Michael's Mount. The great headlands of Land's End and Lizard Point bring you face-to-face with the raging Atlantic Ocean, but you can get closer still by venturing out to the beautiful Isles of Scilly.

St Michael's Mount

10 Sights

1. Tresco Abbey Gardens
2. Pendennis Castle
3. The Barbara Hepworth Museum and Sculpture Garden
4. St Michael's Mount
5. Tate St Ives
6. Minack Theatre
7. St Ives
8. Isles of Scilly
9. Penzance
10. Land's End

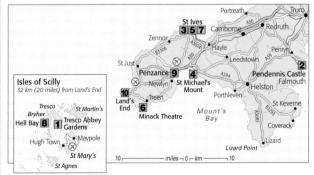

Isles of Scilly
32 km (20 miles) from Land's End

1 Tresco Abbey Gardens

This subtropical oasis on the Isles of Scilly was created in 1834 and nurtured by five generations of the same family. Tresco's unique microclimate and the establishment of tall windbreaks have allowed the gardens to thrive. Currently, over 20,000 plants representing around 200 species from places as diverse as Chile, South Africa and Australia are reared here. Remnants from the ruined priory and modern sculptures create the perfect setting, and there is an interesting collection of ships' figureheads taken from local wrecks *(see pp22–3)*.

2 Pendennis Castle

Fortified by Henry VIII in the 1540s, this formidable castle guarding the Carrick Roads Estuary endured a 5-month siege during the Civil War before falling to Parliamentarian forces. Its stout walls hold the governor's residence, a Tudor fortress in the central keep, and Edwardian and Victorian barracks. Gun rooms contain waxworks, and an outer bastion has an exhibition illustrating the castle's role in World War II. The views from here are terrific. ⬧ *Map C5* • *Falmouth* • *01326 316594* • *Open late Mar–Jun & Sep: 10am–5pm Sun–Fri, Jul & Aug: 10am–6pm Sun–Fri; Oct–Mar & on Sat: 10am–4pm* • *Adm* • *www.english-heritage.org.uk*

An artillery diorama, Pendennis Castle

The Barbara Hepworth Sculpture Garden

3 The Barbara Hepworth Museum and Sculpture Garden

One of the foremost sculptors of the 20th century, Hepworth was inspired by the granite landscape of West Cornwall and settled in St Ives in 1939. Her sleek, abstract sculptures can be seen in her former studio located in the heart of St Ives. The smaller works are displayed inside, but the true glory of the place is the adjoining walled, thickly planted garden – an ideal setting for her large-scale geometric forms *(see p26)*.

4 St Michael's Mount

The dominant feature in Mount's Bay, this castle residence lies a short way out to sea and can be reached by causeway or passenger ferry. The drama of arrival does not end there, for visitors must make a steep climb to reach the house itself. Most impressive among the cosy warren of rooms within are the Tudor Great Hall, with its hunting frieze and the dainty Blue Drawing Room. Other rooms hold armour, weaponry and mementos. The views from the battlements are stupendous *(see pp28–9)*.

There is a concession for joint visits to the Hepworth and Tate Museums.

Boat Trips from Falmouth

Ferries leave for St Mawes from Falmouth's Prince of Wales Pier, all year (1–2 hourly; 20 min). In summer, you can also board boats to Trelissick, Truro (up to 5pm daily) and the hamlet of Flushing on the River Penryn (1–2 hourly), or explore the River Fal and other local estuaries on self-drive cabin cruisers. Check details on www.falriverlinks.co.uk.

Tate St Ives

A beacon of modern art, this gallery pays homage to the local schools of art that flourished in the area, while also showcasing contemporary works, usually with a local connection. Converted from a gasworks in 1993, the building is a modernist statement by itself and is located just across from Porthminster beach. Natural light floods the white-walled rooms, providing an ideal background for the abstract and avant-garde works on display. The rooftop terrace offers stunning ocean views. The gallery closes for several days three to four times a year for hanging, so call before visiting (see p26).

Tate St Ives

Minack Theatre

The vision of one woman, Rowena Cade (see p25), the Minack is a unique attraction in Cornwall. Just like a Roman amphitheatre on some Mediterranean shore, the theatre has been carved out of the cliff-face above the sea, creating a magical setting for watching plays and musicals. Shows are performed over 17 weeks every summer, though the Exhibition Centre is open all year. Contrary to what you might expect, cancellations due to bad weather are rare, but it's advisable to wrap up warmly (see pp24–5).

St Ives

There is a distinctly Mediterranean flavour about this seaside town with its maze of flowery lanes climbing up the hill. This, combined with the clear light and rugged landscape, was a major draw for the succession of artists who settled here, renting studios from local fishermen. Today, tourists have replaced pilchards as the town's mainstay, thronging its sandy beaches, numerous galleries and elegant restaurants every summer. If you wish to escape the crowds, climb up to The Island, a grassy headland with lofty views across St Ives Bay (see pp26–7).

Isles of Scilly

It takes an effort to reach the Isles of Scilly, but few come away disappointed. Imagined by some to be the remains of the lost land of Lyonnesse, the scattered archipelago is breathtakingly beautiful, presenting inspiring vistas in every direction. The beaches here are among the best in the country, but when the sea is up,

The Minack amphitheatre

the best place to be is in Hell Bay, Bryher, to experience the full fury of an Atlantic storm.
🜲 *Map A4*

Penzance
Draped over a hill above a harbour, Penzance has plenty of charm and possesses two of Cornwall's best museum-galleries: Penlee House and The Exchange. All the glories of the Penwith Peninsula are easily accessible from this pleasant town, from the abbey-fortress of St Michael's Mount to the coves and beaches of the rocky coast. For historical character, look no further than the hotels and pubs of Chapel Street and the Art Deco Jubilee Pool *(see pp28–9)*.

Land's End
The western tip of the British mainland has an age-old fascination and offers fine coastal sights. The headland offers panoramic views over the undulating coast and to rocky outcrops out to sea with such intriguing names as the Armed Knight, the Irish Lady and Dr Syntax Head. The Longships lighthouse, 2 km (1.5 miles) out, is also usually visible. Sometimes you can also spot the Wolf Rock lighthouse 15 km (9 miles) to the southwest and even the Isles of Scilly, 45 km (28 miles) away. 🜲 *Map A6*

A Walk from Newlyn to Porthcurno

Morning
🕐 If you're in **Newlyn** early enough, look in on the fish auction that takes place here every morning. Start your walk along a cycle-path running south from the harbour. After about 2 km (1 mile), you will reach the bijou fishing village of **Mousehole** (pronounced "Mowzul"). The place was ransacked by a Spanish raiding party in 1595, who reputedly left just one building standing – the 14th-century **Keigwin House,** which is still visible. Walk through the village and pick up the coast path heading south. You reach **Point Spaniard** where the raiders suppo-sedly landed. The path then swerves inland before meeting the coast again at **Carn Du,** the eastern point of **Lamorna Cove**. Stop for lunch at the **Lamorna Wink** pub.

Afternoon
From Lamorna the path sticks close to the rocky coast. Follow it past **Tater Du** lighthouse and round Boscawen Point to **St Loy's Cove**. Stop at **Cove Cottage** *(see p117)* to try the snacks made with home-grown organic produce. After a short walk, mainly on the clifftop, you will reach unspoiled **Penberth Cove** – little more than a few cottages and fishing boats. Continue along the clifftop, past the Iron Age fort of **Treryn Dinas** *(see p25)*, where you can see the famous **Logan's Rock**. From here the path descends to **Porthcurno**, which has a café and pub, a museum of telegraphy and the **Minack Theatre**.

Left **Grey Seal at the National Seal Sanctuary** Right **Future World @ Goonhilly**

Best of the Rest

1 National Seal Sanctuary
Sick or injured seals are brought to this sanctuary from all over the country. Tour the pools and a specially designed hospital, and view ponies and otters. ✆ Map C5 • Gweek, Helston • 01326 221361 • Open Apr–Oct: 10am–5pm daily; Nov–Apr 10am–4pm daily • Adm

2 National Maritime Museum, Cornwall
This museum in a former boat-yard holds a fascinating variety of vessels and nautical equipment. ✆ Map C5 • Discovery Quay, Falmouth • 01326 313388 • Open 10am–5pm daily • Adm

3 Future World @ Goonhilly
Explore the universe in this satellite station where you can tour the world's oldest working antenna. ✆ Map C6 • 7 miles SE of Helston, Lizard Peninsula • 0800 679593 • Times vary • Adm

4 Jubilee Pool
This open-air Art Deco pool by the harbour is one of the finest examples of Britain's 20th-century lidos, and is ideal for sunbathing (see p28).

5 Geevor Tin Mine
Tour the surface works and the 18th-century tunnels at the UK's largest preserved mining site. ✆ Map A5 • Trewellard, Pendeen, St Just • 01736 788662 • Open Apr–Oct: 9am–5pm Sun–Fri; Nov–Apr 10am–4pm Sun–Fri • Adm

6 The Wayside Museum
This museum has a hotch-potch of more than 5,000 items relating to Cornwall. ✆ Map A5 • Zennor • 01736 796945 • Open May–Sep: 10:30am–5:30pm Sun–Fri (Sat in Aug); Apr–Oct 11am–5pm Sun–Fri • Adm

7 Western Rocks, Isles of Scilly
Boat tours can be taken around these rocks on the fringes of the archipelago. ✆ Map A4

8 The Lizard Lighthouse
This lighthouse on the mainland's most southerly point was erected in 1751, and has distinctive twin towers. ✆ Map C6 • Lizard Point • 01326 290202 • Times vary • Adm

9 Isles of Scilly Museum
Local shipwrecks have contributed many of the exhibits in this museum, which include stuffed birds and art. ✆ Map B4 • Church Street, St Mary's • 01720 422337 • Open Apr–Sep 10am–4:30pm Oct–Apr: 10am–noon Mon–Sat • Adm

10 River Helford
Hire a boat to explore this complex of inlets and shady creeks. Tea rooms along the way provide refreshments. ✆ Map C5

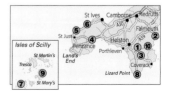

Left **Lanyon Quoit** Right **Men-an-Tol on hills near Penzance**

Prehistoric Sites in West Cornwall

Chun Castle
The walls of this Iron Age hillfort are mainly collapsed, but in parts reach a height of 3 m (9 ft) and the gateposts still stand. The ruined huts inside date from the Dark Ages.
⊛ Map A5 • Near Morvah, off B3318

Chun Quoit
On open moorland, this quoit – a neolithic chamber tomb topped by a flat stone and resembling a giant granite mushroom dates from around 2,000 BC.
⊛ Map A5 • Near Morvah, off B3318

Chysauster
Cornwall's most complete prehistoric monument consists of stone-walled houses arranged around courtyards, where you can discern hearths, basins and drains. ⊛ Map B5 • Near Zennor
• 07831 757934 • Times vary • Adm

Men-an-Tol
The Cornish name (meaning stone-with-a-hole) accurately describes this Bronze Age monument that was long thought to have healing powers. Situated on moorland, it is 2,500–4,000 years old. ⊛ Map A5
• Near Morvah, off Morvah–Madron Road

Lanyon Quoit
Also known as the Giant's Quoit or Giant's Table, this capped burial chamber is one of the most accessible of West Penwith's prehistoric remains.
⊛ Map A5 • Near Morvah

Tregiffian Burial Chamber
This barrow tomb revealed an urn and cremated bones when it was excavated in 1967.
⊛ Map A6 • Near Lamorna, off B3315

The Merry Maidens
Considered Cornwall's most perfect stone circle which, legend has it, is the remains of 19 maidens turned to stone for carousing on the Sabbath.
⊛ Map A6 • Near Lamorna, off B3315

Halliggye Fogou
This is one of the most impressive of West Cornwall's *fogous* – long, underground structures from the Iron Age.
⊛ Map C6 • Trelowarren, Mawgan, Helston • 01326 221224 • Open Apr–Oct

Bant's Carn, Isles of Scilly
One of the Isles' many megalithic monuments, this burial chamber on St Mary's has a roof made of four huge slabs.
⊛ Map B4 • Halangy Down, St Mary's

Porth Hellick Barrow, Isles of Scilly
In the southeastern corner of St Mary's, this is the best preserved tomb in the Scillys'. ⊛ Map B4 • Porth Hellick Down, St Mary's

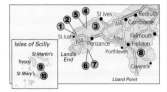

Left **Ship Inn** Centre **Tinners Arms** Right **Admiral Benbow Inn**

Cafés and Pubs

1 Porthgwidden Café
Right above the beach, yet in St Ives' centre, this summer café is ideal for a restorative snack after exposure to sun and sea. ⊗ *Map B5 • Porthgwidden Beach, St Ives • 01736 796791*

2 Gylly Beach Café
A great location on Falmouth's main beach makes this a perfect stop for sandwiches, salads and cold drinks. ⊗ *Map C5 • Cliff Rd, Falmouth • 01326 312884*

3 Pandora Inn
You can reach this remote but scenic spot by road, but it is best approached by river. There are tables right on the waterside for meals or just a pint. ⊗ *Map C5 • Mylor Bridge • 01326 372678*

4 New Inn
This classy pub serves bar snacks as well as lavish feasts. Prices are steep, but less than Tresco's only other eatery and it has outdoor seating. ⊗ *Map A4 • Tresco, Isles of Scilly • 01720 422844*

5 Turk's Head
Considered by island cognoscenti to be the best drinker on the Scillies, this pub is also famous for its pasties. ⊗ *Map A4 • St Agnes, Isles of Scilly • 01720 422434*

6 Blue Anchor Inn
Enjoy the medieval atmosphere at this former monks' resthouse dating from the 15th century. Cosy nooks and home-brewed Spingo ale are the main attractions. Snacks are available. ⊗ *Map B5 • 50 Coinagehall St, Helston • 01326 562821*

7 Admiral Benbow
One of two historic pubs in Penzance's centre, the other being the Turk's Head *(see p58)*, this pub is filled with ship's figureheads and maritime mementos. The restaurant is a ship's galley. ⊗ *Map B5 • 46 Chapel St, Penzance • 01736 363448*

8 Tinners Arms
D H Lawrence was a customer during his stay in Zennor, but the place has been elegantly renovated since then, with bare floorboards and an open fire. Enjoy good ales with the hearty meals served here. ⊗ *Map A5 • Zennor • 01736 796927*

9 Ship Inn
You can almost feel the sea spray in this fisherman's pub above the harbour, full of maritime character. Crab soup and steak-and-ale pie are usually on the menu. ⊗ *Map A5 • South Cliff, Mousehole • 01736 731234*

10 Cinnamon Girl
Falmouth can get quite busy, but you are sure to find peace in this wholefood café in a secluded courtyard. Free Wifi Internet is available. ⊗ *Map C5 • Old Brewery Yard, High Street, Falmouth • 01326 211457*

Price Categories

For a three-course meal for one with half a bottle of wine (or equivalent meal), taxes and extra charges.

£	under £20
££	£20–£35
£££	£35–£45
££££	£45–£55
£££££	over £55

Porthminster Beach Café

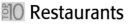 Restaurants

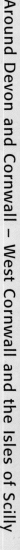

The Abbey Restaurant
Spread over two floors, the Abbey serves quality modern European fare, including game, poultry and fresh seafood. ◈ *Map B5 • Abbey St, Penzance • 01736 330680 • Closed Mon & Sun • £££££*

Harris's
The accent at this restaurant in Penzance's town centre is on fresh local produce, though the dishes are European in inspiration. The light lunch menu is especially good value. ◈ *Map B5 • 46 New St, Penzance • 01736 364408 • Closed Mon & Sun winters • ££££*

2 Fore Street
Head to this relaxed French-style bistro right by the harbour for simple, zesty food such as fish casserole. Enjoy the walled garden in summer. ◈ *Map A5 • 2 Fore St, Mousehole • 01736 731164 • Closed Oct–Apr Mon & Tue • £££*

The Beach
Relax on the terrace here and gaze out over the beach while you dine. The local seafood on the menu adds to the restaurant's attractions. ◈ *Map A5 • Sennen Cove • 01736 871191 • ££££*

Juliet's Garden Restaurant
A casual, modern place above Porthloo Beach with outdoor tables and lovely sea views. Come for a daytime snack or a candle-lit dinner. ◈ *Map B4 • St Mary's, Isles of Scilly • 01720 422228 • Closed Tue & Nov–Mar • ££££*

The Gurnard's Head
This cheerful gastro-inn does a great fish stew among other dishes, such as pilchards and crab. Menus change according to the day's catch. ◈ *Map A5 • Zennor • 01736 796928 • ££££*

Alba
A chic restaurant offering an eclectic range of dishes. Set-price menus are available at lunchtime and early evening. ◈ *Map B5 • Wharf Rd, St Ives • 01736 797222 • ££££*

The Island Hotel
Enjoy superb island vistas at this top-notch hotel and restaurant. Lunches are casual and dinners more formal. Menu items include fillet steak and grilled lemon sole. ◈ *Map A4 • Tresco, Isles of Scilly • 01720 422883 • Evening reservations; closed Nov–Jan • ££££*

The Three Mackerel
Modern Mediterranean cooking is featured at this beach-side place with a panoramic terrace. Tapas is always available and there are barbecues in summer. ◈ *Map C5 • Swanpool Beach, Falmouth • 01326 311886 • Sometimes closes Sun eve in winter • ££££*

Porthminster Beach Café
Beach café by day, smart and pricey restaurant at night, this café serves dishes such as local oysters, scallops and monkfish curry. ◈ *Map B5 • Porthminster Beach, St Ives • 01736 795352 • ££££*

STREETSMART

DEVON AND CORNWALL'S TOP 10

Left **Surf hire shop on Fistral Beach, Newquay** Right **A children's playground**

Planning Your Trip

1. What to Pack

Devon and Cornwall get more sun than any other part of Britain, but be prepared for all kinds of weather. On the coasts especially, the wind can be fierce. Walkers should pack waterproofs. Never underestimate the power of the sun – a sun hat and a good sunscreen are also recommended. Chilly sea temperatures persuade many to swim in a wetsuit which, along with surf equipment and other beach gear, can be rented or bought here.

2. Currency

Most currencies can be changed for British pounds and pence at major banks and main post offices. ATMs are widely found through the region. Credit cards are accepted at most hotels, though many B&Bs will not take them. Sometimes a surcharge is added for credit card transactions.

3. Passports and Visas

Visitors from the Commonwealth and the US do not need a visa for short stays. EU citizens can stay as long as they like. Overseas visitors should check with the British embassy in their home country or their embassy in London to find out more about the visa requirements applicable to them.

4. Customs Regulations

Visitors from most EU countries can bring into the UK as much tobacco and alcohol as they can carry. Those from outside the EU face tighter restrictions but, unlike EU citizens, are entitled to a limited amount of duty-free purchases.

5. Insurance

It is advisable to take out an insurance policy that covers theft, loss of baggage and medical treatment. You can get free emergency treatment at the National Health Service, but specialist care, drugs and repatriation are costly. Keep all receipts for reimbursement. Some policies cover you for lost cash and flight cancellations, though not for injuries sustained in dangerous sports – check with your insurance company for details.

6. Driving Licence

EU citizens can use their driving licence in the UK, but should carry insurance documents and a registration certificate for any vehicle brought into the country. Other foreign nationals need an international licence.

7. Time Difference

Greenwich Mean Time (GMT) is used from late October to late March, when clocks go forward an hour for British Summer Time (BST). GMT is five hours ahead of the US Eastern Standard Time and one hour behind most European countries.

8. Electrical Appliances

The electricity supply throughout the UK is 240 volts AC. Overseas visitors will need a plug adaptor (available in the UK) for any appliances they carry. Most hotels have two-pin sockets for use by shavers only.

9. Children's Needs

Devon and Cornwall are well-supplied for children's amusements and needs. Pharmacies have a range of products for mothers and young children. Although kids are not allowed in some alcohol-serving premises, many pubs have family rooms or beer gardens where they are welcome. Some B&Bs and hotels do not permit kids under a specified age.

10. Membership Cards

Bring any membership cards for driving and heritage organizations that have reciprocal arrangements with UK bodies. The English Heritage and National Trust cards allow free entry into many historical sites. An internationally recognized student card is useful for discounts on transport and sights.

Preceding pages **Diners at Fifteen restaurant**

Left **A train on the Liskeard-to-Looe line** Centre **Camel Trail** Right **King Harry Ferry**

⑩ Getting There and Around

① By Plane
Regular flights connect Devon and Cornwall with many European cities. The region's main airports are in Plymouth, Exeter and Newquay. Land's End Airport has year-round flights to the Isles of Scilly, while Newquay and Exeter only offer flights in summer. British International has helicopter rides from Penzance to the islands.

② By Sea
Plymouth is linked by ferry with France and Spain. Between April and October, ferries cross to the Isles of Scilly from Penzance. In summer, you can reach Lundy Island from Ilfracombe, Bideford and Clovelly. ⑧ *Brittany Ferries: Plymouth; 08712 440744; www.brittany-ferries.co.uk • Isles of Scilly Steamship: Quay St, Penzance; 08457 105555 • Lundy Shore Office: The Quay, Bideford; 01271 863636; www.lundyisland.co.uk*

③ By Road
The region is connected by a good network of roads, though the elongated shape of the peninsula means that most east-west traffic is concentrated along the A30 and A39 roads.

④ By Coach
National Express coaches run up to Penzance with stops at Exeter, Plymouth, St Austell, Newquay, Bodmin, Truro, Falmouth, Helston and St Ives. ⑧ *National Express: 08705 808080 • www.nationalexpress.com*

⑤ By Local Bus
Local buses are a scenic and cheap way to tour the region. Several companies offer passes for unlimited travel over one, three or seven days. Pick up timetables from tourist offices or stations.

⑥ By Train
As well as the main line connecting Exeter, Bodmin, Plymouth, Truro, St Austell and Penzance, branch lines pass through scenic countryside. From Exeter, trains travel south to Exmouth, Torquay and Paignton and north to Barnstaple. From Liskeard, a line heads to Looe. Another crosses to Newquay from Par, and St Erth has a connecting line to St Ives. Call National Rail Enquiries for details. ⑧ *National Rail Enquiries: 08457 484950*

⑦ By Organized Excursion
Many companies offer group travel by coach or minibus. These range from backpackers' buses to luxury coaches. Southwest Tourism will give details (see p108).

⑧ By Local Ferry
Ferry services across rivers and estuaries often save a big detour. The Kingswear Ferry avoids the long route around the River Dart to reach Dartmouth. Passenger ferries operate between St Mawes and Falmouth, Padstow and Rock and, in summer, between Fowey and Mevagissey.

⑨ By Bicycle
You can cycle the whole peninsula. Off-road routes include the Granite Way on Dartmoor, the Camel Trail and parts of North Devon's Tarka Trail.

⑩ On Foot
Most of the region is great for walking. The South West Coast Path encompasses the whole peninsula on its route. Bodmin Moor, Exmoor and Dartmoor are ideal for inland hikes. Tourist offices can provide itineraries (see p108).

Airports

Exeter International Airport
Map L4 • Clyst Honiton, Exeter • 01392 367433

Newquay Cornwall Airport
Map C4 • St Mawgan • 01637 860600

Plymouth City Airport
Map H5 • Crownhill, Plymouth • 01752 204090

Land's End Airport
Map A5 • Kelynack, St Just • 08457 105555

Left **A tourist information centre** Right **Dartmoor National Park information office**

Sources of Information

1 Tourist Information Centres

Every major town – and some villages – has a tourist information centre (TIC) which can supply details of accommodation and activities. Larger offices may also offer an accommodation booking service, either free (you may have to pay at the office and the money is refunded by the hotel or B&B) or for a fee. Most places are open 9am–5pm Monday to Saturday. During summer, many centres stay open on Sundays, while in winter they may have reduced hours or close altogether. ☎ *Southwest Tourism: Exeter • 08704 420880 • www.visitsouthwest.co.uk*

2 National Park Visitor Centres

Dartmoor and Exmoor national parks both have an independent network of visitor centres, which provide useful information services and are a good source of books and maps on the area. ☎ *Dartmoor National Park: Tavistock Road, Princetown; 01822 890414; www.dartmoor-npa.gov.uk • Exmoor National Park: 7–9 Fore Street, Dulverton; 01398 323841; www. exmoor-nationalpark.gov.uk*

3 Websites

All tourist offices have their own local websites. Most hotels, sights and transport companies also have pages where you can book rooms, view information and look up times and timetables.

4 Local Newspapers

Regional newspapers, such as the *Western Morning News* and *West Briton*, usually publish listings for events in the area. They also provide information on local closures, roadworks, tide times and the weather. Magazines such as *Inside Cornwall* and *Devon Life* are useful for cultural coverage.

5 Television

Rooms in B&Bs and hotels that do not offer television are rare. The BBC's Ceefax service has timetables, news and other information.

6 Radio

As with the local press and TV programmes, the radio provides details about events, traffic and the weather. Surfers in particular will find reports on wind and sea conditions especially useful. Tune in to BBC's Radio Devon (94.8, 95.8, 103.4 or 104.3 FM) and Radio Cornwall (95.2 or 103.9 FM) and commercial stations such as Gemini FM (96.4, 97 or 103 FM), Plymouth Sound (97 FM) and Atlantic FM (105–107 FM). These stations can be picked up on digital radio (DAB).

7 Weather

When planning a day out, it is wise to be clued up on the weather forecast. Conditions in the region can change with alarming rapidity and hikers especially can run into the danger by being caught unawares. Fortunately, the region has all-weather attractions, allowing you to plan accordingly. Check the forecast on TV, radio, newspapers, the Internet or at tourist offices.

8 Surf Reports

A host of websites supply up-to-date information on sea conditions for surfers. Try www.a1surf.com or magicseaweed.com.

9 Listings Magazines

Large towns like Exeter and Plymouth have free listings magazines covering large parts of the region. These can be found at tourist offices, pubs or cafés. *247* and *What's On Southwest* are good options.

10 Maps

Road maps of Devon and Cornwall are available in bookshops and at newsagents. If you want more detailed maps, the Ordnance Survey Landranger, Explorer and Outdoor Leisure are recommended. Harvey's maps cover the South West Coast Path and Dartmoor.

Left **An ATM in St Mawes** Centre **Emergency telephone at Logan Rock** Right **A typical post box**

🔟 Banking and Communications

Money
The pound sterling is divided into 100 pence (p). Notes come in denominations of £5, £10, £20 and £50. Coins are 1p, 2p, 5p, 10p, 20p, 50p, £1 and £2.

Banks
Banks are generally open 9:30am–4:30pm Monday to Friday and most have 24-hour external cash machines (ATMs). You can also find ATMs within some food stores and outside supermarkets.

Bureaux de Change
The few independent bureaux de change in Devon and Cornwall are regulated and usually display rates and commission charges. Main post offices change money for no commission. Be sure to compare exchange rates, as these may be unfavourable when commission charges are low.

Credit Cards
Most places accept cards. MasterCard and Visa are common, American Express less so and Diner's Club is rare. B&Bs and smaller campsites may not accept cards, or may ask for a surcharge if they do. Credit cards can be used to withdraw cash from ATMs, but you pay interest from the time of withdrawal.

Postal Services
Post offices are scattered throughout the region, though they may be sparse in rural areas. They open 9am–5:30pm Monday to Friday and 9am–12:30pm or 9am–1pm on Saturdays, with post offices in towns open until 5:30pm. Smaller branches close on Wednesday afternoons. You can buy stamps at newsagents. 🅢 *Post office helpline: 08457 223344 • www.postoffice.co.uk*

Postal Charges
Post offices and the Royal Mail website provide details about postal charges. The rates depend on the size of the package, the destination and time of arrival. For destinations in the UK, letters can be sent first class for next-day delivery or on a cheaper second-class fare for delivery within three working days. Surface mail and express delivery options are also available. 🅢 *Royal Mail: 08457 740740 • www.royalmail.com*

Internet Points
Many hotels, B&Bs and cafés provide Internet service, sometimes for a fee. Some tourist centres have terminals for public use, though often restricted to a few minutes. Towns such as Exeter and Plymouth have Internet cafés charging up to £5 per hour. Public libraries in most towns offer free Internet access, but book in advance. Some phone booths are equipped for email service.

Mobile Phones
Mobiles can be used in most parts of Devon and Cornwall, but some areas are outside signal range, including many coastal and moorland zones. Check before leaving home that your phone works in the UK.

Telephones
Public call boxes found in towns and most villages accept coins (20p minimum) and some take credit cards. It costs at least £2 to make an overseas call, but it is more expensive to call from your hotel. Numbers prefixed by 0800 or 0808 are free, 0845 numbers have local rates and 0870 national rates. 0906 or 0909 numbers cost up to £1.50 per minute. Dial 100 for the operator and 155 for international calls.

Dialling Codes
Omit area codes when calling within the same locality from a land line. When calling from abroad, first dial the access code and then the area code, but omit the initial 0. To call abroad, dial 00 followed by the access code of the country. For directory enquiries, dial 118 500 for domestic and 118 505 for overseas assistance.

Left **Lifeguards on Fistral Beach** Right **Adder, commonly found in the region**

Security and Health

Emergencies
Dial 999 in the event of an emergency. The operator will connect you to the service you need. The call is free from public telephones.

Personal Protection
Provided you follow basic precautions, you are unlikely to encounter any threats. To avoid confrontations with binge-drinkers, bypass pubbing areas on Friday and Saturday nights in resorts such as Newquay and Torquay, and in Plymouth which has a large sailor population. Mugging is rare. It is illegal to carry weapons.

Theft
Petty theft can occur in this region. Valuables are best deposited with your hotel, campsite or B&B hosts. Lock your vehicle and lodge it in a protected car park if you are leaving it for any length of time. Beware of pickpockets in shopping areas and on public transport and don't leave your possessions unattended. If a theft occurs, contact the local police to obtain a crime report number to make an insurance claim.
❧ *Non-emergency contact for police: 08452 777444 (24 hours)*

Lost Property
If you lose any property, contact the local police station, or – if it was lost on a bus or train – the transport company you used.

Ticks and Snakes
Ticks can transmit diseases such as Lyme disease. Small and black, these arachnids can attach themselves to you on moorlands and in wooded areas. To avoid picking one up, cover your arms and legs on walks. If you find one on your skin, consult a doctor or pharmacist promptly. Adders with zigzag markings are the only snakes in the region to beware of. Thankfully they are quite rare. If you are bitten by one, seek medical attention.
❧ *NHS Direct: 0845 4647 • www.nhsdirect.nhs.uk*

Sea Hazards
Weaver fish can be found on some beaches, often lying just below the sand at low tide. Stepping on their poisonous spines in bare feet can cause painful stings. Take precautions by wearing jelly shoes (plastic sandals). Take care not to be stranded by high tides which move in quickly and beware of powerful currents that can sweep you out to sea when you swim. Lifeguards are present on the main beaches.

Hospitals
The hospitals listed below have 24-hour Accident and Emergency departments where you can get treated.
❧ *Royal Devon and Exeter Hospital: Barrack Rd, Exeter 01392 411611 • Derriford Hospital: Derriford Rd, Crownhill, Plymouth; 0845 155 8155 • Royal Cornwall Hospital: Treliske, Truro; 01872 250000*

Pharmacies
Pharmacies, known as chemists in the UK, are present in every town and large village and can advise on minor ailments. Most are open 9am–5pm Monday to Saturday. Many drugs are only available by prescription from a doctor or hospital. Drugs are known by various names in different countries, so if possible, carry a bottle or packet of the drug that you need.

Dentists
Although there are dentists in most towns, few will accept patients who are not registered. In an emergency, call the dental helpline (01872 354375 in Cornwall and 01392 405700 in Devon). If it is after working hours, call 01392 824600.

Women Travellers
There are no inherent problems for female tourists in Devon and Cornwall, though solo travellers should avoid deserted areas at night and not ride in unregistered cabs.

Left **Heavy traffic in the Totnes town centre** Right **Hikers on a coastal path near Porthcurno**

🔟 Things to Avoid

1 School Holidays, Weekends and Bank Holidays

With its beaches and outdoor activities, the region is popular with families, so the best bathing spots and top sights attract throngs. The summer break – between late July and early September – sees the biggest crowds, the least accommodation and the highest prices. Weekends and bank holidays also get uncomfortably crowded. Expect to queue up to visit sights and restaurants. Hotels and B&Bs often require a minimum of two- or three-nights' stay at weekends.

2 Fast Food

Constant snack-breaks can impinge on your budget. The region's resorts are awash with fast-food outlets, and while an ice cream may occasionally hit the right spot, they won't satisfy hunger pangs. Soft drinks are also an expensive way to quench your thirst. Carry a bottle of tap water and some fruit. Make use of the breakfasts offered at your hotel or B&B – they can take you through to lunchtime and beyond.

3 Driving on Saturdays

Saturday is "changeover day" in the West Country, when people in holiday homes on weekly rentals move into or vacate their property. As a result, roads and trains may be packed.

4 Driving in Villages

Many villages are difficult to reach by public transport but with one-way systems and pedestrian areas, they are often tricky to negotiate by car. Fishing villages, especially, cannot handle traffic. Leave your car in a car park, or better still, cycle or walk.

5 Rush Hour

As in every other part of Britain, rush hour can be stressful for drivers and cyclists. In Exeter, Plymouth and Truro, traffic slows completely and country roads too can get congested. Avoid the road between 8 and 9am, and 4:30 and 6pm.

6 Minor Roads at Night

Travelling by road at night not only means you can't admire any scenery that you may pass by, but it can also be dangerous. Coastal roads are often unlit and prone to unexpected twists, while ponies and sheep stray onto unfenced roads.

7 Late Booking of Accommodation

While it may sometimes appear that resorts are full of hotels and B&Bs, availability can get limited during peak times. Campsites and hostels too are booked weeks in advance. Do not count on finding accommodation without a reservation.

8 Saturday-Night Bingers

Devon and Cornwall are no more immune to binge-drinking than other parts of Britain. Most places are perfectly calm, but you may come across rowdy behaviour on weekends. Plymouth, Newquay and Torquay are particularly prone to this, though it is quite rare to encounter any violence.

9 Hiking Without Preparation

Any walk more than a 10-minute stroll should be planned. On the moors and the coasts, the weather can deteriorate quickly; it is not unusual for sunshine to turn to fog without warning. Carry rainproof gear. For longer hikes, carry a map and water, wear stout boots and always inform someone of your route. Remember that often the most scenic areas are out of range of mobile-phone signals.

10 Getting Stranded by Tides

All beaches are liable to be affected by tidal changes. The speed with which a beach can be flooded by high tide is unnerving and it is easy to be cut off from a path back to safety. Take great care wading through fast-moving water.

Left **A harbourside café** Centre **Cycling along the Camel Trail** Right **A town bus in Penzance**

Top 10 Budget Tips

1 Reduced Admissions

Many museums, galleries and sites such as ruined castles are free; if there is a charge, it is usually reduced for children and senior citizens. Discounts are offered for students and the unemployed on production of a card or document. Family tickets (two adults and two kids) are also available.

2 High Season, Low Season and Weekends

Accommodation rates are often higher in peak season and at weekends. However, hotels that primarily cater to business travellers charge less at weekends. Rates are lowest during winter and places such as gardens, whose allure diminishes during winter, also charge less.

3 Hotels and B&Bs

Bed-and-Breakfasts (B&Bs) are usually cheaper than hotels and offer better value. Rates for "short breaks" (three or four nights) are discounted. Hotels and some B&Bs with dining rooms may offer dinner, bed and breakfast packages that are worth considering.

4 Hostels, Bunkhouses, Campsites and Camping Barns

Hostels belonging to the Youth Hostels Association (YHA) offer good accommodation for a fraction of the price of hotels and most have self-catering kitchens. Other hostels, such as surf lodges, are more spartan. Bunkhouses and camping barns with basic facilities exist in rural areas, but early booking is required as they are often rented to groups. Campsites (usually closed in winter), from farmers' fields to well-equipped complexes, are the cheapest option.

5 Train Travel

The more in advance you book your ticket, the cheaper it will be. Same-day tickets are the most expensive, though return tickets can save a few pence. Standard tickets cost less than first class. If you plan on frequent train travel, enquire about Rover tickets which allow unlimited travel over a specific period.

6 Bus and Coach Travel

Buses (for short-distance trips) and coaches (for cross-country runs) are cheaper than trains, but take longer. National Express, the main long-distance coach operator, offers discounted "fun fares" for specific journeys booked in advance (see p107). Megabus also offers cheap fares for journeys between London, Exeter, Plymouth and Newquay. Locally, individual bus companies offer money-saving Explorer tickets. Contact Traveline for details. 🛈 *Megabus: 09001 600900; www.megabus.com • Traveline: 08712 002233; www.traveline.org.uk*

7 Walking and Biking

The cheapest way to get around is on foot or by bike. The coast path, in particular, is a wonderful resource for travelling by foot. Most train companies carry bikes for free, but some require prior booking; it is worth doing so, as bike-carrying capacity is limited.

8 Eating Out

If you are eating out, you can save a great deal by opting for places offering set-price menus, especially at lunchtime and before 7pm.

9 Self-Catering

Apartment and cottage rentals are usually cheaper than hotels and B&Bs as they offer self-catering facilities. Campsites have washing-up areas, but no kitchens, nor do they encourage open fires for cooking, though barbecues are allowed.

10 Markets

The West Country has markets where you can buy fresh produce at low prices. Clothes are also sold. Enquire about these at the local tourist office (see p108).

Left **A dinghy** Centre **Surfing at Woolacombe Bay** Right **Photographing the coastline**

10 Specialist Holidays

1 Cultural Holidays
You can take in everything from Tudor mansions to art colonies on organized tours lasting a day or stretching over a week. Other interests include field trips to explore the region's archaeological heritage, seafood cookery courses, and painting courses. Accommodation is in places that reflect the subject, such as historic hotels or artist-run B&Bs.

2 Touring Holidays
Devon and Cornwall offer several attractions that can be sampled on regular coach tours from London, Exeter and Plymouth. With all accommodation arranged for you, sit back and enjoy the scenery.

3 Walking Holidays
Whether on riverside strolls or moorland hikes, walking is one of the main attractions of the West Country. Joining an organized group provides structure, company and expertise in the form of knowledgeable guides. The cheapest and easiest option would be to hook up with the small groups that venture daily onto Dartmoor on circular walks lasting three–six hours. For longer hikes, companies arrange guides and accommodation at select hostels, hotels or B&Bs along the way. Baggage is transported independently.

4 Cycling Holidays
A network of cycleways allows you to explore the region at your own pace. Operators supply bikes, itineraries and maps and arrange overnight stops. Mountain bikes, bikes for kids, tandems and trailers are all available, as are helmets and child-seats. Favourite routes include Devon's Tarka Trail and Cornwall's Camel Trail *(see p36)*. Most of the routes are flat, with numerous stops possible at pubs and picnic spots. Bike rental outfits deliver and collect bikes to and from your hotel.

5 Surfing Holidays
The region has some of Britain's best surfing beaches. Several companies cater to enthusiasts – the majority are in Newquay, the "surf capital". They offer boards, wetsuits and tuition by qualified instructors, and some cater to women-only groups.

6 Riding Holidays
Dartmoor and Exmoor in particular are popular areas for treks, but stables are also scattered across the whole region, with direct access to riding terrain. Rides are for people of all abilities and lessons are available.

7 YHA Holidays
The Youth Hostels Association (YHA) is the biggest provider of activity holidays. Many of its hostels provide courses over weekends. While most hostels are fully modernized, some offer accommodation in basic camping barns.
⊗ *Youth Hostels Association* • 08707 708868; outside UK 01629 592700 • www. yha.org.uk

8 Sailing Holidays
The more sheltered southern seaboard of Devon and Cornwall is ideal to mess about in boats. Companies based in Dartmouth, Salcombe, Plymouth and Falmouth provide all the know-how you need. You can learn the ropes on basic dinghies or join the crew of a restored sailing ship.

9 Wildlife Holidays
Devon and Cornwall are a wildlife-lover's haven, offering rich opportunities for anyone interested in hawks, owls, otters or snakes. The estuaries in particular hold some of the nation's rarest species of waders and wildfowl. On sea safaris, you can get close to seals, dolphins and basking sharks.

10 Adventure Holidays
The region offers action-packed adventure holidays for every taste, either adult-only or for families. Instructors teach basic survival skills on weekend multi-activity courses.

Contact Southwest Tourism (08704 420880; www.visitsouthwest.co.uk).

Left **Garrack Hotel** Centre **Bovey Castle** Right **Hotel Tresanton**

🔟 Luxury Hotels

1 Garrack Hotel
This family-run hotel is a steep climb up from St Ives and offers state-of-the-art gym facilities with a pool and sauna. Most of the rooms have ocean views and the restaurant is top-notch. 🚫 *Map B5 • Burthallan Lane, St Ives • 01736 796199 • www.garrack.com • ££££*

2 Island Hotel
With its private beach and sailing school, this jet-setters' hideaway could well be in some tropical location. Most of its spacious rooms have balconies or terraces offering views over the rock-strewn sea. The restaurant makes good use of local seafood. 🚫 *Map A4 • Tresco, Isles of Scilly • 01720 422883 • Closed Nov–Feb • www.tresco.co.uk • £££££*

3 Burgh Island Hotel
This palatial structure set on its own island is a testament to Art Deco elegance. Its curves and turret give it the appearance of an ocean-liner, while the interior is reminiscent of the Jazz Age. Facilities include a rock pool and helipad. 🚫 *Map J6 • Bigbury-on-Sea, Devon • 01548 810514 • www.burghisland.com • £££££*

4 Hotel Tresanton
An ex-yachting club, this hotel has rooms decorated with Cornish art, most offering panoramic views over the Carrick Roads Estuary. There is a cinema and an Italian-inspired restaurant here. Guests can use the yacht and speedboat in summer. 🚫 *Map C5 • 27 Lower Castle Rd, St Mawes • 01326 270055 • www.tresanton.com • £££££*

5 Combe House
Country-house elegance does not come any better than this luxurious retreat. The tone is more intimate than formal, and the bedrooms are plush. There are plenty of nooks for curling up with a book and wildflower meadows to wander through. 🚫 *Map L3 • Gittisham, Devon • 01404 540400 • www.thishotel.com • ££££*

6 Gidleigh Park
This romantic haven at the end of a narrow lane in Dartmoor, has traditional rooms decorated with antiques and equipped with modern gadgetry. The restaurant is one of the region's best (see p81). 🚫 *Map J4 • Chagford, Devon • 01647 432367 • www.gidleigh.com • £££££*

7 Hotel Endsleigh
A former hunting lodge transformed into an island of opulence by the team responsible for the Tresanton. Each of the 16 rooms is different, but have all been restored to their Georgian appearance. A stretch of the River Tamar runs through the estate. 🚫 *Map H4 • Milton Abbot, Tavistock • 01822 870000 • www.hotelendsleigh.com • £££££*

8 Lewtrenchard Manor
This secluded Jacobean manor house boasts oak-panelled rooms, stone fireplaces and sleigh beds in the bedrooms. The restaurant uses ingredients from home-grown produce to prepare meals. 🚫 *Map H3 • Lewdown, Okehampton • 01566 783222 • www.lewtrenchard.co.uk • ££££*

9 Bovey Castle
Surrounded by a majestic parkland, this mansion has stately, well-equipped rooms. Activities include tennis, a spa and an 18-hole golf-course. The afternoon tea is recommended. 🚫 *Map K4 • North Bovey, Dartmoor, Devon • 01647 445016 • www.boveycastle.com • £££££*

🔟 St Martin's on the Isle
Resembling a cluster of granite cottages, this top-class hotel has rooms overlooking the Scilly seascape. Meals at the Michelin-starred Teän are outstanding. The hotel can arrange boat trips and snorkelling. 🚫 *Map B4 • St Martin's, Isles of Scilly • 01720 422090 • www.stmartinshotel.co.uk • £££££*

Price Categories

For a standard double room per night, inclusive of taxes and any additional charges.

£	under £65
££	£65–£100
£££	£100–£150
££££	£150–£200
£££££	over £200

Gurnard's Head

TOP 10 Seaside Hotels

The Slipway Hotel
There is a real sense of getting away from it all in this quayside hotel in a typical Cornish village. Some of the rooms look out onto the water, just a stone's throw away. The hotel has a good restaurant and cheerful bar. Parking is some way up the hill. ◈ Map D3 • Harbour Front, Port Isaac • 01208 880264 • www. portisaachotel.com • £££

Gurnard's Head
The seven rooms of this inn are simply furnished with feathery-soft beds. Stripped floors and open fires add to the ambience. There is not a lot of space but the setting is spectacular and the food in the restaurant is heavenly (see p103). ◈ Map A5 • Zennor, Cornwall • 01736 796928 • www. gurnardshead.co.uk • £££

The Red Lion
Dominating Clovelly's small harbour, the antique Red Lion hotel has a nautical flavour. The rooms, though small, have wonderful sea or harbour views. Guests can use a lane at the back of this traffic-free village to reach the hotel. ◈ Map G2 • Clovelly • 01237 431237 • www. clovelly.co.uk • £££

Shelley's
Named after the poet Percy Bysshe Shelley who is said to have stayed here, this hotel offers spacious rooms with good views. The river glides by on one side and you can explore the steep gorge behind the hotel. Breakfasts are generous and tasty. ◈ Map J1 • Lynmouth, Devon • 01598 753219 • www. shelleyshotel.co.uk • £££

Driftwood Spars
Relics from shipwrecks went into the construction of this 17th-century building. Most of the rooms offer sea or garden views. One of the hotel's three bars has live music at weekends. ◈ Map C4 • Trevaunance Cove, St Agnes, Cornwall • 01872 552428 • www. driftwoodspars.com • ££

Saunton Sands Hotel
The stunning location above the beach is the biggest draw of this clifftop hotel. There are indoor and outdoor pools, tennis courts and country paths for excursions. Insist on a room facing the sea. ◈ Map H1 • Braunton, Devon • 01271 890212 • www.brend-hotels.co.uk • £££££

Pier House Hotel
Superbly positioned on the quayside, this hotel offers comfort and charm. There is a bistro and a formal restaurant serving delicious food and a pub next door. The South West Coast Path passes directly outside and the Eden Project (see pp10–11) is only a few minutes' drive away. ◈ Map D4 • Charlestown, St Austell, Cornwall • 01726 67955 • www.pierhouse hotel.com • ££

The Harbour Hotel
All the five rooms in this converted Victorian house have balconies and offer amazing views over Newquay's harbour. The restaurant offers alfresco dining. Early booking is essential. ◈ Map C4 • North Quay Hill, Newquay, Cornwall • 01637 873040 • www. harbourhotel.co.uk • £££

Imperial Hotel
This stately pile on a height above the sea exudes splendour, with its chandeliers, marble floors and a formal ambience. Bedrooms are spacious – it is worth paying extra for a front-facing one with a superb view. ◈ Map K5 • Park Hill Rd, Torquay • 01803 294301 • www.barcelo-hotels.com • £££

Whitesands Hotel
Located above Sennen Cove, this hotel is popular with surfers. Each room has a world city theme, such as "Washington" and "Nairobi". As well as an elegant restaurant, the hotel has hammocks in the garden and hosts barbecues in summer. ◈ Map A5 • Sennen, Cornwall • 01736 871776 • www. whitesandshotel.co.uk • ££

Left **Hotel Barcelona** Centre **Q Restaurant, Old Quay House Hotel** Right **Royal Seven Stars Hotel**

Town Hotels

Abbey Hotel
Antiques, books and smouldering fires make this 17th-century hotel a real find. A few rooms at this "shabby chic" place have superb views over St Michael's Mount.
⌂ Map B5 • Abbey St, Penzance • 01736 366906 • www.theabbeyonline. co.uk • ££££

Hotel Barcelona
The wonderfully quirky Hotel Barcelona was converted from an old eye hospital and is filled with retro pieces. The fully equipped rooms are plush and there is a bistro-restaurant offering Mediterranean dishes and a late-night lounge in the basement. ⌂ Map Q3 • Magdalen St, Exeter • 01392 281000 • www. aliashotels.com • £££

Browns Hotel
Sophisticated Browns Hotel has elegant rooms, modern art on the walls and a clubby atmosphere. Breakfast includes orange juice, free-range eggs and organic bread, while the restaurant serves evening meals and tapas. ⌂ Map K5 • 27–9 Victoria Rd, Dartmouth • 01803 832572 • www.brownshotel dartmouth.co.uk • £££

Royal Seven Stars Hotel
This atmospheric coaching inn in the centre of town has been modernized but retains its 17th-century charm. Rooms come with en-suite showers and have WiFi access. The hotel has a restaurant and two bars serving snacks. ⌂ Map K5 • The Plains, Totnes • 01803 862125 • www. royalsevenstars.co.uk • £££

Royal Hotel
This central hostelry has a contemporary feel and is ideal for a night or two in Cornwall's capital. The rooms are individually designed and apartments are also available. The bar and grill serves Mediterranean-style food. ⌂ Map C5 • Lemon St, Truro • 01872 270345 • www.royalhotel cornwall.co.uk • £££

Abode Exeter
Locally known as the Royal Clarence, one of the country's oldest hotels has been modernized and boasts fully equipped rooms. Its main draw is its location opposite Exeter Cathedral and the Michael Caines' restaurant (see p81). ⌂ Map P2 • Cathedral Yard, Exeter • 01392 319955 • www.abodehotels.co.uk • £££

The Old Quay House
Truly the lap of luxury, this hotel is original in tone. As the name suggests, it is right on the water, with big windows and a sun terrace taking advantage of the vista. Rooms are opulent – those with river views cost more. The restaurant is one of Cornwall's best. ⌂ Map E4 • 28 Fore St, Fowey • 01726 833302 • No under-12s • www.theold quayhouse.com • ££££

Union Hotel
This Georgian hotel has decor in keeping with the period. Rooms are neither fancy nor modern, but are perfectly adequate for the price. Breakfast is served in old assembly rooms. ⌂ Map B5 • Chapel St, Penzance • 01736 362319 • www. unionhotel.co.uk • ££

Browns
Located on the edge of Dartmoor, this coaching inn has been refashioned into a boutique hotel and has a brasserie, courtyard and conservatory. The small rooms have the latest gadgetry. ⌂ Map H4 • 80 West St, Tavistock • 01822 618686 • www. brownsdevon.com • £££

Bowling Green Hotel
This hotel next to Plymouth Hoe has comfortable beds in good-sized rooms. The tasty breakfast will set you up for the day. Secure parking is a bonus in Plymouth. ⌂ Map P6 • 9–10 Osborne Place, Lockyer St, The Hoe, Plymouth • 01752 209090 • www.bowlingreenhotel. com • ££

Streetsmart

116

Price Categories

For a standard double room per night, inclusive of taxes and any additional charges.

£	under £65
££	£65–£100
£££	£100–£150
££££	£150–£200
£££££	over £200

Mason's Arms

🔟 Budget Hotels and B&Bs

1 The Old Rectory
This rural guest house on Boscastle's outskirts was the place where author Thomas Hardy stayed. All rooms are preserved in their Victorian splendour and there are lovely wooded gardens. ✆ *Map E2 • St Juliot, Boscastle • 01840 250225 • Closed Dec–mid-Feb • No under-12s • www.stjuliot.fsnet.co.uk • ££*

2 East Dyke Farmhouse
A 15-minute walk above the honeypot of Clovelly, this 200-year-old farmhouse has three spacious bedrooms equipped with fridges and private bathrooms. There is a flagstoned dining room for hearty breakfasts served around a large table. ✆ *Map G2 • Higher Clovelly, Devon • 01237 431216 • No credit cards • £*

3 Rock Cottage
At the western end of Sidmouth's Esplanade, this B&B is an Edwardian *cottage orné* typical of the region. Two of the three spacious rooms offer sweeping sea views and there is also a sun terrace. ✆ *Map L4 • Peak Hill Rd, Sidmouth • 01395 514253 • www.rockcottage.co.uk • ££*

4 Mount Tavy Cottage
This B&B set in a lush garden is a great base for walkers. Guests can sleep in a 250-year-old gardener's cottage or in two garden studios. Generous breakfasts are served and evening meals are available by prior arrangement. Bring your own wine. Self-catering accommodation is also offered. ✆ *Map H4 • Tavistock, Devon • 01822 614253 • www.mounttavy.freeserve.co.uk • ££*

5 Cove Cottage
With a coastal path running past the bottom of the garden, Cove Cottage will appeal to walkers. However, it may be hard to venture outside – the one room available is of majestic proportions with sofas, underfloor heating and stunning views. ✆ *Map B5 • St Loy, St Buryan, Penzance • 01736 810010 • Closed Dec–mid-Feb • No credit cards • Two-night minimum stay • £*

6 Treverbyn House
This Edwardian guest house up from Padstow's harbour has spacious rooms with open fires and wooden or cast-iron beds. Breakfast is served in the room or on a terrace with river views. Parking is available. ✆ *Map D3 • Station Rd, Padstow • 01841 532855 • No credit cards • www.treverbynhouse.com • ££*

7 Garlands
This cheerful B&B a few minutes up the hill from Porthmeor Beach and the Tate has three colourful rooms, a family-room and a shared bathroom. ✆ *Map B5 • 1 Belmont Terrace, St Ives • 01736 798999 • No credit cards • Minimum 3-night stay in Jul & Aug • £*

8 Lower Norton Farmhouse
A secluded retreat deep in the countryside, this Georgian house features three plush bedrooms, and offers organic breakfasts, candlelit evening meals and a tour in a vintage Bentley. ✆ *Map K5 • East Allington, Totnes • 01548 521246 • No credit cards • www.lowernortonfarmhouse.co.uk • ££*

9 Mason's Arms
One of the prettiest villages in East Devon boasts this exceptional inn. The traditional rooms range from the grand, with beamed ceilings, to smaller options. The food is gourmet and the setting idyllic. ✆ *Map L4 • Branscombe • 01297 680300 • www.masonsarms.co.uk • ££*

10 Pengilley Guest House
This simple B&B is close to the main town beach and has six tastefully decorated rooms. Breakfasts feature home-grown produce. ✆ *Map C4 • 12 Trebarwith Crescent, Newquay • 01637 872039 • No credit cards • www.pengilley-guesthouse.com • £*

Left **Boscastle YHA** Centre **Reef Surf Lodge** Right **Falmouth Lodge**

TOP10 Hostels and Bunkhouses

1 Sparrowhawk Backpackers

Well-placed for excursions to Dartmoor, this hostel has dormitories in a converted stable and double rooms in the main house. A large kitchen is at the disposal of guests, though exclusively for vegetarian cooking. Pubs and restaurants are a brief stroll up the street. ⚲ Map J4 • 45 Ford St, Moretonhampstead • 01647 440318 • www.sparrow hawkbackpackers.co.uk • ££

2 Falmouth Lodge

This scrupulously tidy hostel down a quiet street is close to the railway station. There is a TV lounge, well-equipped kitchen and dining room. Bunkrooms and private rooms are available. ⚲ Map C5 • 9 Gyllyngvase Terrace, Falmouth • 01326 319996 • www.falmouth backpackers.co.uk • £££

3 Lizard YHA

Located on Britain's most southerly point, the Lizard YHA is one of the best YHA hostels. Choose between dormitory rooms or a family room. Cooking and washing facilities are available. ⚲ Map C6 • Lizard Point, Cornwall • 08707 706120 • www.yha.org.uk • £££

4 Boscastle YHA

This hostel on Boscastle's quayside was all but washed away during a flash flood in 2004. Now restored, it provides excellent accommodation in one of Cornwall's loveliest spots with coast walks on either side. You can sleep in the small dormitories or the family rooms. ⚲ Map E2 • Palace Stables, Boscastle • 08707 705710 • Open late-Mar–early-Nov • www.yha.org.uk • ££

5 Okehampton YHA

Housed in a converted railway goods shed on the northern edge of Dartmoor, this hostel caters to a gamut of pursuits including rock climbing, gorge scrambling, pony trekking and archery. Camping is also possible. ⚲ Map H3 • Klondyke Rd, Okehampton • 08707 705978 • www. yha.org.uk • ££

6 Old Chapel

One of Cornwall's most attractive independent hostels occupies an old Methodist chapel in a village where D.H. Lawrence once lived. There is a good café, and packed lunches and evening meals are available. Dramatic coastal walking is close at hand and the hostel has family rooms. ⚲ Map A5 • Zennor, Cornwall • 01736 798307 • www.zennorbackpackers. co.uk • ££

7 Plume of Feathers

At the heart of Dartmoor, this pub in the oldest building in Princetown runs a couple of bunkhouses with cooking facilities, showers and a day room. Other options include B&B and camping. ⚲ Map J4 • Princetown, Dartmoor • 01822 890240 • www.theplumeof feathers.co.uk • ££

8 Runnage Farm

This cattle and sheep farm near Bellever Forest offers the choice of sleeping in camping barns on raised wooden areas, bunkrooms or camping. A kitchen and showers are provided for. Bikes are available for hire. ⚲ Map J4 • Postbridge, Yelverton • 01822 880222 • www.runnagecamping barns.co.uk • ££

9 Reef Surf Lodge

One of Newquay's best hostels, this boasts upmarket facilities. All rooms are fitted with TVs and have bathrooms. Surf packages are a speciality, and there is live entertainment. ⚲ Map C4 • 10–12 Berry Rd, Newquay • 01637 879058 • www.reefsurf lodge.co.uk • £££££

10 North Shore

Surfers make a beeline for this hostel with 12 rooms including en-suite doubles. There is a kitchen for self-catering and barbecues in summer. Internet facilities are available. Doubles cost more. ⚲ Map E2 • 57 Killerton Rd, Bude • 01288 354256 • www.northshore bude.com • ££

Price Categories

For a dormitory bed	£	under £10
or a standard	££	£10–£15
camping unit for two	£££	£15–£20
people and a pitch.	££££	£20–£25
	£££££	over £25

Ayr Holiday Park

🔟 Campsites

Ayr Holiday Park
The only campsite in St Ives situated above Porthmeor Beach has terrific sea views. It is pricey but clean and has a solar-powered shower block. The town centre is just a kilometre (half a mile) away. ✎ *Map B5 • Ayr Terrace, St Ives • 01736 795855 • www. ayrholidaypark.co.uk • £££££*

Little Meadow
This campsite is located on one of the most scenic stretches of North Devon. Facilities are minimal but include a modern shower block. Footpaths lead to the beach and Watermouth Castle. ✎ *Map H1 • Watermouth, Ilfracombe • 01271 866862 • Closed Oct–late Mar • www.little meadow.co.uk • £££*

Carnon Downs
One of the few options open all year, this large site between Truro and Falmouth is sheltered. Though much of the space is given to motor homes, the facilities are excellent and pubs are within walking distance. ✎ *Map C5 • Carnon Downs, Truro • 01872 862283 • www.carnon-downs-caravanpark.co.uk • £££*

Dennis Cove
Simplicity is the keynote at Dennis Cove, situated alongside the Camel Estuary. The location above the Camel Trail makes it a useful base for anyone wanting to explore this walking and biking route. ✎ *Map D3 • Dennis Lane, Padstow • 01841 532349 • Closed Oct–Mar • ££*

Bryher Campsite
You cannot get much further off the beaten track than at this stripped-down site on the Isles of Scilly. The island views are magnificent. The Fraggle Rock café-pub is close by. ✎ *Map A4 • Bryher, Isles of Scilly • 01720 422559 • Closed Oct–Mar • www. bryhercampsite.co.uk • £*

Tamar Valley Tipis
For a novel take on camping, stay in authentic tipis in a wooded site in the Tamar Valley. Colourful rugs adorn the interior where beds are laid out along the circumference. There is a central wood-burning stove and a barbecue. Bring your own bedding and food. ✎ *Map G5 • Deer Park Farm, Luckett, Callington • 08454 560302 • Closed Nov–Mar • www. tamarvalleytipis.co.uk • £££££ per week*

North Morte Farm
Close to Devon's top surfing beaches, this hilly site is not very sheltered, but has knock-out views over to Lundy. A footpath leads down to a rocky beach while the lovely Woolacombe beach is a 2-km (1-mile) walk away. As it is an extensive site, it very rarely seems over-crowded. ✎ *Map H1 • North Morte Rd, Mortehoe, Woolacombe • 01271 870381 • Closed Oct–Apr • www. northmortefarm.co.uk • £££*

Broad Meadow House
Accommodation at this site is in family-sized tents, which houses up to eight people. Pitches for camping with your own tent, a B&B and a self-catering lodge are also available. ✎ *Map D4 • Quay Rd, Charlestown, St Austell • 01726 76636 • Closed Oct–Apr • No credit cards • www.broad meadowhouse.com • £££££*

Lundy Island Campsite
One of the country's bleakest campsites with modern facilities. Diving and climbing are among the activities to be pursued on the island. ✎ *Map G1 • Lundy, Devon • 01271 863636 • Closed Mar–Nov • www. lundyisland.co.uk • ££*

South Penquite
On the outskirts of Bodmin Moor, this eco-friendly site has spacious pitches and four Mongolian yurts. Futons provide comfort, but you have to carry your own sheets. ✎ *Map E3 • Blisland • 01208 850491 • Closed Nov–Apr • www. southpenquite.co.uk • £*

General Index

Acknowledgments

The Author

Robert Andrews has been travelling and writing travel guidebooks for 20 years. His main areas of interest are the West Country in England and southern Italy. Based in Bristol, he also writes articles, compiles anthologies and takes photographs.

Publisher
Douglas Amrine

List Manager
Christine Stroyan

Managing Art Editor
Mabel Chan

Senior Editor
Sadie Smith

Senior Designer
Paul Jackson

Project Editor
Ros Walford

Senior Cartographic Editor
Casper Morris

Picture Researcher
Ellen Root

DTP Operator
Natasha Lu

Production Controller
Rita Sinha

Photographer
Nigel Hicks

Fact Checker
Kate Hughes

Maps
Maps by JP Map Graphics Ltd. based on data from the People's Map.

Picture Credits
t-top, tl-top left; tc-top centre; tr-top right; cla-centre left above; ca-centre above; cra-centre right above; cl-centre left; c-centre; cr-centre right; clb-centre left below; cb-centre below; crb-centre right below; bl-bottom left, b-bottom; bc-bottom centre; br-bottom right.

Works of art have been reproduced with the kind permission of the following copyright holders: Barbara Hepworth Sculpture Garden with *Four Square (Walk Through)* 1966 © Bowness, Hepworth Estate 97tr.

The Publisher would like to thank the following individuals, companies and picture libraries for their kind permissions to reproduce their photographs:

ALAMY: Peter Barritt 23tl; Andrew Besley 6cl; David Chapman 8cb, 8br; Patrick Eden 26–7c; geophotos 34tr; Glenn Harper 34bc; Paul Heinrich 38tl; Graham Lawrence 38tr; Mary Evans Picture Library 56tr; National Trust Photolibrary/Derek Croucher 8cl; National Trust Photolibrary/Andreas von Einsiedel 9cr; National Trust Photolibrary/John Hammond 8tr; National Trust Photolibrary/Derek Harris 9bc; National Trust Photolibrary/Claire Takacs 50b; National Trust Photolibrary/ Geraint Tellem 56bl; Pontino 35tl; The Print Collector 56c. CORBIS: Rune Hellestad 11tl; E.O. Hoppe 56tl; Hulton-Deutsch Collection 57tl; Skyscan 28–9c.

FIFTEEN CORNWALL: Ben Rowe 104–5.

NATIONAL TRUST PHOTOLIBRARY: John Bethell 29bl; Andreas von Einsiedel 9tc, 14crb; Jerry Harpur 8–9c.

NIGEL HICKS: 7tl, 22cl, 22cb, 22crb 22–3c, 23bl, 23cr.

PHOTOLIBRARY: Peter Barritt 32–3; David Noton Photography 88–9; Robert Harding Travel 4–5; Thomas Dobner-Dartmoor Collection 72–3.

TATE ST IVES: Barbara Hepworth Sculpture Garden Photo © Bob Berry 97tr.

Special Editions of DK Travel Guides

DK Travel Guides can be purchased in bulk quantities at discounted prices for use in promotions or as premiums. We are also able to offer special editions and personalized jackets, corporate imprints, and excerpts from all of our books, tailored specifically to meet your own needs.

To find out more, please contact:
(in the United States) **SpecialSales@dk.com**
(in the UK) **travelspecialsales@uk.dk.com**
(in Canada) DK Special Sales at **general@tourmaline.ca**
(in Australia) **business.development@pearson.com.au**

Selected Town Index

Index